Best Restaurants New York

By Stendahl

101 Productions
San Francisco

Copyright, 1978, 101 Productions, Inc.

Printed in the United States of America.
All rights reserved.

Best Restaurants is the trademark of Critic
Publishing Company, Inc., registered with the
United States Patent and Trademarks Office.

Published by 101 Productions
834 Mission Street
San Francisco, California 94103

Distributed to the book trade in the United States
by Charles Scribner's Sons, New York

Library of Congress Cataloging in Publication Data
Stendahl.
   Best restaurants New York.

   Includes index.
   1. New York (City)–Restaurants–Directories.
I. Title.
TX907.S728   647'.95747'1   78-9420
ISBN 0-89286-137-1

Contents

INTRODUCTION 4
NEW YORK CITY: MANHATTAN 6
NEW YORK CITY: OTHER BUROUGHS 184
   The Bronx 185
   Brooklyn 186
   Queens 190
THE ENVIRONS OF NEW YORK 195
   Long Island 196
   Putnam County 211
   Westchester County 212
   Ulster County 216
   Northern New Jersey 217
INDEX 218

Introduction

Only love, dreams and films are more subjective than dining out. Aware that one man's fish is another man's *poisson*, I have seized the tureen by the handles and made this an extremely personal book.

New York has in excess of 10,000 tablecloth restaurants. Had the limit for this book been set at 200 instead of a little over half that many, the challenge would have been less formidable. However, eight years on radio and in the press as a professional diner-out gives me the courage to stand by my choices.

It is true that New York is a little world, and probably offers a wider choice of ethnic dining than any other city on earth. I have chosen from among this profusion of gustatorial offerings those establishments which I believe best provide enjoyable dining experiences in many styles and price ranges.

My chief criteria for a restaurant have always been quality and consistency, in both food and service. In my years as food critic for WCBS-NY and *The New York Daily News*, my procedure has remained the same. I visit a restaurant anonymously, I always pay my own way, and I always try to visit a place several times so I can be sure of my evaluation. I take pains to listen to colleagues, but the final decision is purely my own.

To keep this book manageable, where there have been several restaurants of the same type and price category, I have selected the one I prefer. To the few of my favorites I have omitted for one reason or another, my apologies. If I have omitted one of yours, please send me a report (in care of this publication or to Stendahl, Box A, Sea Cliff, New York 11579) and I'll investigate it before our next edition.

Prices do not long remain steady in New York, so our system of rating is to be taken only as a relative guide. Prices quoted in this book were in effect at the time of publication and are subject to change at any time.

$ **UNDER $10.** Good food in plain surroundings. Casual service.

$$ **UNDER $20.** In the range between $10 and $20 you may expect professional service and some ambience, as well as superior food.

$$$ **OVER $20.** In this range you should expect—and demand—excellent food, exceptional ambience, and service that is impeccable.

These price ranges were determined on the basis of the average cost of a three-course meal; tax, tip and beverages not included.

New York City: Manhattan

View of Manhattan from Trinity Church Steeple, 1872.

Manhattan: Midtown West
APERITIVO
Northern Italian

$$$

Chianti flasks hang in rows and on the walls are slogans in half-a-dozen languages. Tables are nearly always full, abuzz with business, romance and gossip. The host, Paul, bounces between groups, lingering longest wherever there is a pretty woman. Steaming plates heaped high flow from the kitchen, while corks pop to celebrate an extensive and interesting wine list that favors bottles from the Tyrol to Sicily. Soups are thick and heady. Pastas are exceptional, particularly when Paul makes up one of his trilogies that might combine green and white tagliatelle, little nuggets of tortellini and a perky spaghetti carbonara. Most of these fine pastas are made by Paul's wife and are a best buy at $6.25. Scampi are sometimes too tough to justify a steep $10.50, but you won't go wrong on any of the veal dishes. A house specialty that supposedly draws clients from as far away as Seattle is the special broiled veal chop. At $12.50 it is a bargain, about a full pound of juicy, flavorful, snow-white veal. On Tuesdays, or by advance order, there is also a monumental *osso buco,* heaped high and red-glowing as a chimney. The rugola and endive salad, pretty as a still life, is a marvel of crispness and bittersweet tastes. And no one gets out of Aperitivo without the frothy, tangy Key lime pie that Paul's wife makes. It caps a superior meal in a roisterous, hospitable establishment.

APERITIVO, 29 West 56th Street, Manhattan. Telephone: (212) 765-5155. Hours: 11:30-3, 5:30-10:30, Monday-Friday; 5:30-11, Saturday; closed Sunday. Cards: AE, BA/Visa, DC. Reservations required. Parking in nearby garages. Full bar service.

Manhattan: Midtown West
ARIRANG HOUSE
Korean $$

It strikes me as strange that Korean cuisine has not caught on more with Americans, since it is founded on what Americans dote on: beef. There are about half-a-dozen Korean establishments in various parts of midtown, but Arirang was the first and remains as good as any. Waitresses look like butterflies in filmy native Korean dress, which appears to these eyes as a type of negligee. The butterflies are helpful with translations and suggestions as far as their English permits. Decor is humble Oriental. A combination appetizer plate is a good way to begin. It offers several taste treats, such as *wanja* (savory little meatballs) and little beef egg rolls called *mandu*. The classic Korean soup is *mandu kuk*, again the little egg rolls in a beef broth. *Pul koki* (*bulgoki* in some restaurants) is marinated beef strips grilled at tableside. *San juk* is a shish kebab. Another classic is *kalbi kui*, lean short ribs of beef marinated in a piquant sauce and broiled. Complete dinners featuring these traditional items, or chicken or shrimp, plus vegetables, rice and beverage list at $10.95 and similar complete lunches are about $5. For the adventurous there are unusual listings such as *sin sullo*, a hot pot of beef, chicken and vegetables placed for individual fishing right on your table. Vegetable items include seaweed and the blistering and essential condiment, *kimchi*, fire-spiced pickled cabbage and turnips.

ARIRANG HOUSE, 28 West 56th Street, Manhattan. Telephone: (212) 581-9698. Hours: 12-2:30, 5-10:30, Monday-Friday; 5-10:30, Saturday; closed Sunday. Cards: AE, BA/Visa, CB, DC, MC. Reservations suggested. Parking in nearby garage. Full bar service.

Poultry

DAK KUI (BROILED CHICKEN) **6.25**
Breast, thigh, and leg of spring chicken marinated and broiled.

DAK TUIKIM (Southern Fried CHICKEN) 6.25
Spring chicken fried as only the South Koreans know how.

DAK CHIM (CHICKEN SWEET SOUR)... 6.25
One half fried chicken simmered in Korean wine sauce with exotic spices and seasonings.

Specialties

SIN SULLO **7.95**
A specialty of the House, literally "The Angels Brazier." The brazier containing a hearty pot of pourri of beef, chicken, mushrooms and vegetables is placed piping hot on the table and served leisurely and individually.

YAUK HAE (STEAW TARTAR) **6.95**
Finely ground sirloin, marinated and seasoned with sesame. This gourmet delight is served raw and with a very unusual sauce.

CHAPCHAE **5.75**
Transparent noodles smothered with mushrooms and various lightly cooked vegetables, topped with julienne sirloin of beef.

SAM HAPCHO **6.95**
Shrimp abalone, and sirloin tips combined with carrots, sweet chestnuts, seaweed, celery, and mushrooms in a sweet and sour wine sauce. DELICIOUS!

Manhattan: Midtown East
AUBERGE SUISSE
Swiss $$

If you like Jean-Luc Godard films, you'll love the decor of Auberge Suisse, in the below-ground Citicorp complex. It is easy to become pleasantly disoriented by the two-level dining area with its geometric patterns, reflective foil ceiling and peek-through partitions. Somehow, the decor is not at all in keeping with what is actually a very nice, neat little French-Swiss restaurant. The single drawback of the place is that, like it or not, one must dine leisurely, partly because the hostess often deserts her post to clear tables, leaving waiting customers stranded. Most dishes at Auberge Suisse are so beautifully presented that one hesitates to destroy them with a fork. Outstanding for both beauty and taste is *filet de sole Tessinoise,* delicate fish on a bed of fresh tomato, Gruyère cheese and lightly done spinach. And I can find no fault with the *emince de veau Zurichoise,* a cream-sauced sweet white veal, topped with thin-sliced fresh mushrooms and adorned with first-rate *rösti* potatoes, the pancake golden and crusty outside, moist within. The traditional fondue of Gruyère cheese is served for two, and is authentic though expensive at $16. Desserts are picture-pretty, especially the *champignon glacé,* a meringue fantasy that simulates a mushroom, accompanied with ice cream and a rich hot chocolate sauce. Entrées, served with salad, are $7 to $11.50. **Dezaley,** at 54 East 58th Street, is a sister restaurant to the Auberge Suisse. It shares the same owner-chefs but offers a few Swiss specialties of its own that the all-French Auberge menu lacks.

AUBERGE SUISSE, 153 East 53rd Street, Manhattan. Telephone: (212) 421-1420. Hours: 12-2:30, 5-10, Monday-Saturday; 12-6, Sunday. Cards: AE, BA/Visa, CB, DC, MC. Reservations suggested. Parking in nearby garage. Full bar service.

ENTREES

Emincé de veau Zurichoise 11.50
Zurich's famed veal geschnetzeltes in mushroom cream sauce with rosti potatoes

Plat Bernois 10.00
Traditional Bernese hot plate. Smoked meats, bauernwurst, boiled beef and sauerkraut

Saucisse de veau grillé 7.00
St. Gallen style veal sausage with rosti potatoes and braised onions

Fondue Vaudoise 16.00
A piquant all Gruyere cheese fondue for two

Filets de sole Tessinoise 8.50
Gruyere and tomato topped fillet of sole on a bed of leaf spinach

Truite aux hérbes 8.50
Trout poached in white wine with herbed cream sauce

Tournedos cordon-rouge 11.00
Filet mignon, foie gras, prosciutto, Bearnaise sauce and mushroom with port wine gravy

Suprême de volaille en croûte 8.50
Breast of chicken baked in a pastry crust with tomatoes and Gruyere cheese

Foie de veau 9.00
Calf's liver with chippolata sausage and sauteed pear

All entrées served with salad

Manhattan: Lower Midtown
BALKAN ARMENIAN
Armenian

$

There are many Middle Eastern restaurants in New York, but only a few are Armenian. This is the version of tomato-eggplant-lamb cuisine I like the best, and the Balkan Armenian has a traditional approach to this aromatic kind of cooking. Some people who have never eaten Armenian food know of the owners: Ed Berberian narrates a droll series of radio commercials for his restaurant, proclaiming it as "possibly the oldest continuing Armenian restaurant in the world." Sister Kathie is a noted and musically daring mezzo-soprano. Those who have not eaten here have missed one of the ageless taste treats in New York. The place itself is nothing to look at, being purely functional. Waiters are apt to have that abstraction of old pros who have been around for years, but they get the food on the table while it is still hot. One of my favorite dishes, *doener kebab* (the divine inspiration for the commercial, omnipresent gyro gyro) is obtainable only at lunch, as is another old-time

---

AJEM PILAF: **4.95**
Tasty morsels of tender Lamb molded on Pilaf with Chick Peas and savory BALKAN gravy.

KABAK DOLMA: Delicately stuffed Zucchini squash...Armenian style. (With home-made MADZOON....70 extra) **4.95**
KOUZOU DOLMA: Baked Lamb served on exquisitely flavored Fancy Pilaf. **5.25**
KOUZOU KEZARTMA: Portion of baked Lamb served with Prinz Pilaf. **5.25**

MANTAR (MUSHROOM) KEBAB: **5.95**
Superb preparation of Lamb smothered in Mushrooms, Green Peppers and Onions.

PATLIJAN KAZAN: Sautéed Eggplant chunks served with Baked Lamb. **5.50**

preference, *harpoot kufte,* unusual meatballs of cracked wheat and lamb, stuffed with minced lamb and pine nuts, served in a tasty broth. Dinners offer a choice of 10 exotic olive oil-drenched appetizers and 19 main courses. A special seven-course dinner may be made up from everything by adding $3.75 to the price of any entrée. A not-to-be-missed dessert is *ekmek kadayiff,* a sinfully syrupy toasted pastry topped with *kaymak,* an incredible chilled condensed cream. As to the main dishes, I am forever amazed at how different the combinations of lamb, rice and eggplant can be made to taste. Everything is cooked by Mama Louise Berberian and is worth trying once. What more could anyone want, except low prices? And the Balkan Armenian has those, too. À la carte luncheon and dinner entrées are in the $5 range.

BALKAN ARMENIAN, 129 East 27th Street, Manhattan. Telephone: (212) 689-7925. Hours: 12-2:30, 4:30-9, Monday-Friday; 4:30-10:30, Saturday; closed Sunday. Cards: AE, BA/Visa, DC, MC. Reservations suggested. Street parking. Full bar service.

PATLIJAN KARNI YARIK: 5.60
Generous portion of Eggplant filled with choice minced Lamb, Pignolia and fresh Tomato.

PATLIJAN SILKME: Sautéed Eggplant chunks with pot-roasted pieces of Lamb 5.50
TASS KEBAB: Tender chunks of Lamb, pot-roasted in rich savory BALKAN gravy. Served with Prinz Pilaf 5.25
TOURLU GUVECH: Selected portion of baked Lamb smothered in superbly prepared mixed garden-fresh Vegetables 5.95
BAMYA GUVECH: Selected portion of baked lamb smothered in fresh okra à la mode de BALKAN 5.95
HAHVY (CHICKEN) DOLMA: Roast half chicken on a bed of fluffy Fancy Pilaf 5.50

YAPRAK SARMA: 5.50
A truly delectable preparation of vine leaves stuffed with meat and rice.
(With home-made MADZOON ... .70 extra)

Manhattan: Midtown East
BOX TREE
French $$$

A famous Box Tree restaurant in England inspired a Box Tree in upper New York, which in turn inspired a Box Tree in midtown Manhattan. The result is French food prepared with gentlest care and served with understated British aplomb, adding up to one of the most delightful dining experiences that a tired metropolis can offer. At the Box Tree, the kitchen is so small that the dishwasher has to step outside to let the chef pass. Nonetheless, from this miniscule space comes superb food, served in a dainty, beautiful dining room. (Beautiful, but bad for a hulking figure like Stendahl, whose notorious elbows simply cannot be placed on a table more suited for a backgammon board.) In the main room is art nouveau stained glass paneling in soft woodland colors, and glimmering copper buckets filled with fresh fruits. Service is as quietly considerate as if one were supping in an English country manor. A specialty, *mousse de haddock fumé,* is an ethereal white cloud, smokily perfumed. Stendahl's Choice is the *crème de fenouil,* a memorable cream soup based on that too-neglected delicacy, fresh fennel. Six main dishes are offered which do not often change, but are always expertly prepared, and beautiful in presentation. Their famous dessert, *vacherin* Box Tree, a frothy creation of meringue, chantilly and fresh fruit, is preceded by complimentary cheeses and a glass of tawny port. No bargains on the wine list, but the carefully selected bottles are served with respect. Luncheons are *prix fixe* at $16; dinners $27.

BOX TREE, 242 East 50th Street, Manhattan. Telephone: (212) 758-8320. Hours: 12-3, 6-12, Monday-Friday; 6-12, Saturday-Sunday. No credit cards. Reservations required. Parking in nearby garage. Wine and beer only.

Manhattan: Upper West Side
CAFE DES ARTISTES
Continental/Eclectic

$$

One of the most delightful dining spots in Manhattan, Cafe des Artistes recaptures the spirit of a romantic rendezvous of the 1930s. Naively nude murals by Howard Chandler Christy are replicated by artful placement of mirrors in the elegant dining room. The menu is on the whole quite good, and is definitely imaginative. There is a zestful sense of adventure surrounding a huge service table, laden with first courses and fanciful desserts, plunked in the center of the busy place. The sum is excitement to the eye and palate. On command, a waiter brings to your table two little wine carriers, four whites in one, four reds in the other. Any or all of them are yours for only $8 each, and there are occasionally estate-bottled gems among them. Menus change daily. First courses have included dazzlingly good cream soups, a chilled gazpacho with a base of baby shrimp and a fine array of charcuterie, mostly made by the cafe's chef. Main dishes I've enjoyed here have been perfect, pink lamb chops with béarnaise; trout with walnuts; and moist but non-fatty duckling with apples and Calvados. Pastas are interesting but usually overcooked. Desserts stagger the eye, the palate and the calorie count: the notorious Ilona chocolate torte, frozen mocha and praline cake, sensational pecan-packed pie and a chocolate mousse cake that is the ultimate for chocaholics. Best of all, many samples are piled together on The Great Dessert Plate at $3.95. There is a single *prix fixe* daily dinner at $12.50, luncheons are about $8.50, and the rest is à la carte.

CAFE DES ARTISTES, 1 West 67th Street, Manhattan. Telephone: (212) TR7-3500. Hours: 12-3, 5:30-11:30, Monday-Friday; 5:30-11:30, Saturday; 12-3 (brunch), 4-8, Sunday. Cards: AE, BA/Visa, DC, MC. Reservations required. Parking in nearby lot. Full bar service.

Manhattan: Upper East Side
CAFE DU SOIR
French $

This old-timer up in Yorkville has for many years served excellent country food at prices that everyone can afford. Once through the modest entrance, you are in a French world. Past the strictly neighborhood bar and into the long narrow dining area in the back, you find cheerful waitresses. Walls are of dark brick with imitation shuttered windows looking out on painted French countryside scenes. The food is simple but carefully prepared, and will remind you of that little auberge where you dined last summer near Toulouse. An interesting French pumpernickel is a good bread to match the peasanty soups. Plates are brought to the table quite hot, as they should be. A house specialty is *tranches de noix de boeuf maison,* three tender slices of beef, trimmed of every vestige of fat, covered with a delicious brown sauce. In season, a venison steak with sauce chevreil is unusual in that you can order it rare if you wish. The duckling is tender and nicely seasoned, although, alas, the rice that comes with it is nondescript. As if to counterbalance this, the waitress brings a pony of Cointreau to flame your duck at tableside. Vegetables are served in separate side dishes, a welcome touch, and they are usually very good. Wines are well priced, many under $10. There are no great estates, but there is a St. Emilion '73, a Château Simard '71 and a good Alsatian Sylvaner. An unusual Basque liqueur, Izarra, a variation on the Chartreuse theme, is worth sampling. In all, there are 16 complete dinners available here for under $10. A record hard to match.

CAFE DU SOIR, 322 East 86th Street, Manhattan. Telephone: (212) AT9-9996. Hours: 12-12, Tuesday-Sunday; closed Monday. Cards: AE, BA/Visa, CB, DC, MC. Reservations suggested. Street parking. Full bar service.

DINNER

Price of the Entree Determines Price of the Dinner

Dinner Includes — Appetizer · Soup · Entree · Salad · Dessert · Beverage

APPETIZERS

Hore D'Oeuvres Varies	Coquille Saint Jacques
Pate Maison	Bismark Herring
Crepe Farcie	Fruit Cup
Jambon de Bayonne	Assiette Du Chef
Tomato Juice	Imported Sardines
Salami De Gene	Oeuf A La Russe
Tomates Aux Filets D'Anchovies	Coeurs d'Artichauts Vinaigrette
Half Grapefruit	Maquereaux Au Vin Blanc
Saumon Fume 1.75	Shrimp Cocktail .... 2.00 Extra
Cherrystone Clams 1.25	

Escargots De Bourgogne (6 pieces) 2.75 Extra

SOUP

Onion Soup — Consome en Tasse — Potage Du Jour

POISSONS

FILET OF SOLE MEUNIERE	7.00	9.25
SHRIMPS MODE CAFE DU SOIR	8.75	11.00
TRUITE DE RUISSEAU, Amandine	6.25	8.50
FROG LEGS SAUTE PROVENCALE	10.25	12.50
SCAMPIS, Garlic Sauce	9.95	12.25

ENTREES

TRANCHES DE NOIX DE BOEUF MAISON	7.00	9.25
LE COQ AU VIN DE CHAMBERTIN	6.25	8.50
VEAL SCALOPPINE AU MADERE	7.25	9.50
ROGNONS DE VEAU, Marchand de Vin	6.25	8.50
SLICED FILET OF BEEF, Mushroom Sauce	9.75	12.00
HALF DUCKLING FLAMBE, Sauce Bigarrade	7.50	9.75
CERVELLES AU BEURRE NOIR	6.50	8.75
FRENCH POT ROAST A La Bourgeoise	6.25	8.50
STEAK SAUTE BORDELAISE	8.95	11.25
RIS DE VEAU A L'ARIEGEOISE	8.50	10.75
TRIPES A La Mode de Caen	6.90	9.25
BOEUF BOURGUIGNON	7.50	9.75
CALF'S LIVER & BACON	7.25	9.50
POULET CHASSEUR	6.25	8.50

GRILLADES

BROILED SPRING CHICKEN	6.25	8.50
PORK CHOPS, Apple Sauce	6.25	8.50
LONDON BROIL DU CHEF	6.25	8.50
LAMB CHOPS GRILLE VERT PRE	9.75	12.00
FILET MIGNON, Aux Champignons	11.75	14.00
PRIME SIRLOIN STEAK	11.50	13.75
(Special) ENTRECOTE For Two	23.50	28.00

All Entrees Served with Fresh Vegetable, Potatoes and Salad

DESSERTS

Manhattan: Yorkville
CAFE GEIGER
Viennese/German $

Yorkville, once famous as Little Germany, has become in recent years a hodgepodge of cultures, and all character is now threatened by an invasion of fast-food shops. But a classic example of New York German cooking and baking in the old spirit remains. Cafe Geiger, subtitled "Vienna Pastry Shop," still pours out platters of schnitzels, mountains of schlag, and piles of strudels and tortes. Young people in search of hearty food at affordable prices mingle with genteel oldsters from the Old Country, reminiscing over their imported *trauben-apple,* Johannisbeer *saft,* or schlag-topped coffee while they munch their *schwarzwalder kirschtorte* (kirsch-flavored cake), rigo square (chocolate-cream cake) or one of the other rich and richly decorated tortes or pastries. The menu spans an amazing range. Homemade head cheese, *ochsen maul* (ox cheek salad) and an Hungarian goulash soup that is a chunky meal in itself are among the openers. Then there are *eisbein* (fresh pig's knuckle with sauerkraut and potatoes), many schnitzels, sausage dishes and substantial entrées such as *roulade* of beef (seasoned beef slices, stuffed with bacon, pickles and onions, served with red cabbage and potatoes). There are potato pancakes, apple pancakes and German pancakes. And more. Entrées are priced from $3.65 to $8.95, salad included, for both lunch and dinner. Look in the glass case of the bakery as you enter and pre-select a dessert; you'll never have courage for it later.

CAFE GEIGER, 206 East 86th Street, Manhattan. Telephone: (212) 734-4428. Hours: 9 am-midnight, Sunday-Friday; until 2 am, Saturday. Cards: AE, BA/Visa, CB, DC, MC. Reservations suggested. Street parking. Full bar service.

Entrees

BROILED LAMB CHOPS, VERT PRE	8.25
Tender young lamb chops with herb butter	
BROILER HALF SPRING CHICKEN SERVED WITH APPLE SAUCE	4.65
CHOPPED SIRLOIN OF BEEF	4.50
Freshly chopped prime beef steak with crisp onions or mushroom sauce	
KASSLER RIPPCHEN	5.95
Smoked loin of pork with sauerkraut and choice of potatoes	
EISBEIN - Fresh pigsknuckles with sauerkraut and potatoes	4.15
BROILED JERSEY PORK CHOPS - With Potatoes and applesauce	5.60
BRATWURST OR BAUERNWURST - With sauerkraut and potatoes or with potato salad	3.75
WIENER WUERSTCHEN	3.65
Vienna style frankfurters with sauerkraut and potatoes or with potato salad	
OUR SPECIALTY: JAEGER SCHNITZEL	6.25
Delicate veal cutlet, Hunter's style, in brown mushroom sauce	
SCHNITZEL A LA HOLSTEIN	6.50
Sauteed veal cutlet with fried egg, capers and anchovies	
WIENER SCHNITZEL	5.75
Breaded veal cutlet sauteed in creamy butter	
SAUERBRATEN, BAVARIAN STYLE	5.75
Marinated prime eye round of beef with potato dumpling and red cabbage	
ROULADE OF BEEF	5.75
Delicious seasoned slices of beef, rolled and stuffed with bacon, pickles and onions, served with red cabbage and your choice of potatoes	
FRESH GENUINE CALF'S LIVER	6.25
Broiled or sauteed with bacon or onions	
VEAL SCALLOPINI AU MARSALA	6.50
Tender slices of veal in Marsala wine and mushroom sauce	
PORK FILET A LA PICATTA - Pan fried in a batter of eggs and parmesan cheese	5.95
ROAST LONG ISLAND DUCKLING (15-20 Minutes)	6.25
Crisp and golden brown with orange sauce	
BROILED PRIME SIRLOIN STEAK - With choice of potatoes, vegetable and salad	8.95
VIENNA ROASTBRATEN - Minute steak marinated with mustard, topped with crisp onions	7.95
GERMAN PANCAKE - Served with whole cranberry sauce or apple sauce	3.40
APPLE PANCAKE WITH CINNAMON SUGAR (20 minutes)	3.40
POTATO PANCAKES WITH APPLE SAUCE (20 minutes)	3.30

Manhattan: Upper East Side
CARLYLE RESTAURANT
Continental

$$$

Recently the Hotel Carlyle reorganized itself and overhauled its kitchen and menus. Bemelmans' cartoons were removed from one section of the grand old bar, and this now-stodgy nook, renamed The Gallery, serves tea and dainties. Bemelmans' impudent sketches, however, still adorn the walls of the bar itself. The Carlyle Restaurant is a plush three-room scene: The first room is intimate, with five little tables surrounded by gentle Oriental hangings, and the rear room with six tables is decorated in restrained black and white. My preference is the central room with about 14 tables, and a grand center area with greatly overstuffed seats where you dine looking out over the rest of the room. Dinners are à la carte. Among the entrées is a topnotch *carre d'agneau,* in which the pink-red lamb is cut steak-style and laved in its juice. Vegetables are always skillfully done; desserts are typical of the French cuisine and well turned out. Luncheon features such entrées as roast chicken with tarragon, London broil and cheese soufflé. Dinner will easily cost $20, lunch about $10. On Sunday there is a lavish brunch for $9.50, featuring fresh fruits and items that range from chicken curry with *pappadums* and condiments, to hash of prime ribs of beef, to buckwheat or blueberry pancakes and, of course, eggs. In the hotel there is also the Cafe Carlyle, an elegant snackery and night club that, at this writing, is home for the bouncy Bobby Short. The Cafe also serves buffet luncheons daily and Sunday brunch.

CARLYLE RESTAURANT, 45 East 76th Street, Manhattan. Telephone: (212) 744-1600. Hours: 12-3, 6-11, daily; Sunday brunch, 12-3. Cards: AE, CB, DC. Reservations suggested. Parking in hotel garage. Full bar service.

Les Potages

Le Potage du Jour 2.25
Consommé 2.00 Vichyssoise 2.50
Bisque de Homard 3.75 Petite Marmite 2.75

Les Poissons

Fresh Brook Trout Carlyle 10.50 Striped Bass Provençale 11.25
Seafood à la Nage 10.75 Escalope de Saumon à l'Oseille 10.25
Crab Meat Dewey 12.50 Filet de Boston Sole à Votre Choix 8.75

Les Entrees

Le Plat du Jour 11.75
Côte de Veau aux Morilles 15.75
Foie de Veau Anglaise 10.50
Poulet Rôti à l'Estragon 9.50
Ris de Veau aux Petits Pois 10.50
Mignonettes de Boeuf aux Primeurs 13.75
Escalope de Veau au Citron 10.75
Carré d'Agneau Printanière (2 pers.) 32.00
Canard Montmorency (2 pers.) 26.00

Les Grillades

Steak au Poivre 18.00 Sirloin Steak 17.50
Filet Mignon 16.50 Côte d'Agneau 13.50
Minute Steak 14.50 Demi Poulet Grillé 9.50

Manhattan: Midtown West
CHARLEY O'S
Irish Pub
$$

If you overlook all the non-funny quips and slogans, and the martini-clutching madness of the lunch hours, you will find quite good food at quite good prices. And the Sunday brunch is one of the most serious in all Manhattan. Most self-respecting persons interested in dining out would X-out Charley O's if they forced their way into the stampeded herd that mills around during the day. On Sunday and at nights, the place becomes a restaurant I respect for the quality of its simple unadorned cuisine. Servings are more than ample, meats are first-rate and so are the desserts. Corned beef and cabbage is just the way it should be. Barbecued beef bones and Irish lamb stew are also good. Fried jumbo prawns in ale batter have their champions, and any true Irishman would approve of the Irish fries, potato shells, and Irish potato pancakes. Definitely save room for desserts. You may want to venture into the Irish coffee sweets, such as Bassett's Irish coffee ice cream, a hot fudge Irish coffee sundae or a luscious homemade Irish coffee pie. There are also Irish coffee drinks worth exploring, Irish tea and beers and ales worth quaffing. Main courses, à la carte, are priced from $6.95 to $13.95.

CHARLEY O'S, 33 West 48th Street, Manhattan. Telephone: (212) 582-7141. Hours: 12-2 am, Monday-Saturday; 11-3 brunch, 5-10, Sunday. Cards: AE, BA/Visa, CB, DC, MC. Reservations suggested. Parking in nearby garage. Full bar service.

Charley O's
BAR & GRILL & BAR

"Solid drink
and good food.
That's my theory."

Main Courses

Charley O's CORNED BEEF and CABBAGE   7.25
IRISH LAMB STEW   6.95
THICK PRIME SIRLOIN STEAK   12.95
SLICED BEEFSTEAK on TOAST   7.95
GRILLED CHOPPED STEAK   6.95
ROAST PRIME RIBS OF BEEF   11.95
BRANDIED SKILLET STEAK   13.95
BARBECUED BEEF BONES   6.95
LAMB CHOPS   11.95
CALF'S LIVER with Onions   7.50
CHICKEN POT PIE   7.25

Seafood

FISH OF THE DAY   7.50
SCALLOPS BROILED OR FRIED   7.50
FRIED JUMBO PRAWNS
   IN ALE BATTER   7.50
FISH AND CHIPS   6.95

Manhattan: Midtown East
CHATEAU RICHELIEU
French
$$$

From the bar to the two large dining rooms, decor at Le Richelieu is sumptuous. Walls are rose damask, and filtered light glows like sunset from behind colored glass. Fresh flowers are on every table. The overall sound level is as discreet as the lighting. Impeccable waiters insure prompt service, yet one never gets a feeling of being rushed. Soups are excellent, and I like the way they are served from metal bowls, with a second helping kept hot at the warming table. There is a price-fixed dinner at $20 that includes a wide range of hors d'oeuvre and potages, and a choice of nine entrées, plus dessert and beverage. Selections from the à la carte menu will quickly exceed that sum. In addition to classic and near-classic French cuisine, there are a few worthwhile Italian dishes. My favorite among these is the risotto (either Milanese, with saffron; or if you are fortunate, Piemontese, with white truffles). No bargain at $14, but a delectable gustatorial experience nonetheless. Carefully prepared veal and beef dishes range from $12 to $16 for a too-rich but impressive *tournedos Rossini*. The wine list indicates abundance in the cellar, and while there are few bargains, the bottles are well priced. Appellation controlée wines may be had by the glass, a civilized touch. I wish that more *haute cuisine* establishments would follow suit. Desserts are lavish, rich, and in keeping with the elegance of the Cardinal's Château.

CHÂTEAU RICHELIEU, 48 East 52nd Street, Manhattan. Telephone: (212) PL1-6565. Hours: 12-12, Monday-Saturday; closed Sundays and major holidays. Cards: AE, BA/Visa, CB, DC, MC. Reservations necessary. Street parking after 7 pm. Full bar service.

MENU DU DINER

Les Hors d'Oeuvres

Hors d'Oeuvre Assortis
Le Demi Pamplemousse au Kirsch
La Coupe de Fruits Frais
Le Salami Italien Les Coeurs d'Artichauts
Le Pâté du Chef aux Pistaches
Le Melon (en Saison)
Les Sardines Portugaise
Marinated Herring
Les Blue Points, Les Cherrystones ou Les Little Necks sur Glace
Les Jus: V-8, Tomate, Pamplemousse ou Clam

OU

Les Potages

Potage du Jour Consommé au Vermicelle La Soupe à l'Oignon
Le Consommé en Gelée La Vichyssoise Froide
Consommé Madrilène

Les Entrees

LES BAY SCALLOPS aux AMANDES
LE RED SNAPPER GRILLÉ BEURRE BLANC
LES SUPRÊMES de SOLE DIPLOMATE
LA BOUILLABAISSE RICHELIEU
LES PICCATA ou MARSALA de VEAU
LES MIGNONETTES de BOEUF SAUTÉES aux ECHALOTTES
LE CANARD à l'ORANGE
LE POULET de GRAIN SAUTÉ au CHAMPAGNE
LES MEDAILLONS de VEAU NORMANDE

Served with Potatoes and Vegetable or Salade Maison

Desserts au Choix

Crème Caramel Mousse au Chocolat Glace ou Sorbet
Pâtisserie du Cardinal Fraises au Sabayon Cheese Cake
Le Plateau des Fromages

Café Thé Sanka Filtre

Prix du Diner — $20.00

Manhattan: Midtown West
CHEZ NAPOLEON
French $

This tiny place is such a delight I almost wish I could keep it secret. It is as close to an authentic bistro as you are likely to find in New York. Its out-of-the-way location is a benefit in any case, since there are so many regulars here that, if the place were more accessible, there would be a long line outside. Literally outside, for the only waiting room at Chez Napoleon is on the sidewalk. However, if you make a reservation and are punctual, the efficient staff will see that you are promptly taken care of. Now, this is not Paris, but Brittany. Dining here is like dining in a French family home. Mama presides over the tiny bar and everything else that goes on. Papa is king of the kitchen, invisible as he turns out splendid honest fare. And the waitresses are among the happiest and most charming in the city, eager to make sure you get everything you want, and on hot plates, too. Down-home prices mean that you can get a satisfying lunch for under $5, and an ample dinner below $10. The Stendahl Choice here is *lapin au vin blanc,* tender rabbit done in a sauce that demands sopping up. *Boeuf bourguignonne* is also robust and richly sauced. Lamb chops are served plain, but the meat is excellent. Fish is always fresh. Your waitress will undoubtedly come back to your table to ask if you don't agree that everything is really good. On some occasions, they slip a little bowl of extra gravy to their favorite customers. The wine list is as tiny as the restaurant, but they are all decent wines at budget prices. A final nice touch: If anyone asks for a liquor not stocked at the bar, Madame makes sure that next time he visits, he will find his heart's desire waiting for him.

CHEZ NAPOLEON, 365 West 50th Street, Manhattan. Telephone: (212) CO5-6980. Hours: 12-2:30, 5-10, Monday-Friday; 5-10:30, Saturday; closed Sunday. Cards: AE, BA/Visa, MC. Reservations necessary. Street parking. Full bar service.

Manhattan: Upper East Side
CHEZ PASCAL
French $$$

In this neat little town house, charm glows like a warm hearth. Original paintings of quality adorn the walls (including one surprising porno bit), wood and red brick are subtly lit, and chairs have graceful oval wicker backs. Service is quiet and impeccable by a staff that genuinely cares. The chef apprenticed at famed Taillevent in Paris, and the menu shows it. In the modern manner, dishes are based on classics but have their own accent: *Médaillon de veau, morilles,* for example, is handsome and outstandingly delicious, but its sauce is darker and more earthy than the usual light cream. Béarnaise is slightly spicy, and so is a hollandaise maltaise, with orange peel shreds added for texture and sharpness. A house pride is Chez Pascal's version of bouillabaisse, a gargantuan platter of seafood topped by a spread-eagled lobster is brought forth with a steaming bowl of broth. There is a single special dinner each night at $24.50 and the rest is à la carte, with main dishes ranging from $14.50 to $17.50. *Escargots en croûte* at $5.25 is typical of prices for hors d'oeuvre. One of the best dishes on the menu is an unusual *truite farcie au champagne,* trout stuffed with a bit of crabmeat, then napped with an airy champagne sauce. That piquant béarnaise is served with a moist grilled salmon, and there is also a *suprème de bass au Chablis.* Desserts are not exciting; best is a lemon pie made intriguing by grainy lemon zest. The impressive wine list ranges from a Château Latour '61 for $65 down to a Simard '71 at $14.

CHEZ PASCAL, 151 East 82nd Street, Manhattan. Telephone: (212) 249-1334. Hours: two sittings nightly at 7 and 9:30. Cards: AE. Reservations required. Street parking. Full bar service.

Manhattan: Chinatown
CHINA ROYAL
Cantonese
$

Since the craze for Szechwan and Hunan cooking has taken hold, it has become difficult to find authentic Cantonese food, valued by old China hands as the subtlest of Chinese cuisines. Wonderfully authentic is China Royal and food is king. The atmosphere is nothing special. Walls glitter with waterfall scenes, lights are bright, rushing waiters seem indifferent but are highly efficient, and if you bring your own wine it is served in a water glass. But almost every dish plunked down is striking enough to be photographed, and taste matches appearance. Even with three floors there is apt to be a wait for a table. On weekends, when they serve their amazing array of *dim sum* (steamed dumplings), there may even be a line outside at 8:00 am. Banquets are usually staged on the upper floors, and these are my favorite spots. Great round tables are packed with Chinese families—everyone from grandpa to the latest infant—celebrating a wedding, a reunion or a holiday. Peering at the laden tables I get new ideas about what to order, for there are always mouth-watering masterpieces that go unnoticed on the seven-page menu. Special banquet menus for five to 10 persons are priced at a modest $8 to $10 per person. Stendahl's Choice is a section on the regular menu labelled "Tai Leung Specialty." These dishes feature a delectable creation called "fried milk," a crunchy essence resembling a non-sweet, deep-fried custard. My favorite is fried milk with spareribs in Peking sauce. There are many exotic items, too, such as pomelo peel with shrimp roe and stewed frog with bitter melon. Dishes range from $2 to $6 à la carte.

CHINA ROYAL, 17 Division Street, Manhattan. Telephone: (212) 226-0788. Hours: 8 am-midnight, daily; dim sum, Saturday-Sunday, until 2 pm. No credit cards. Reservations for banquets only. Parking in nearby garage. Bring your own wine or beer.

Manhattan: Midtown East
CHRIST CELLA
Steakhouse $$$

Many experienced diners claim Christ Cella is New York's finest steakhouse. I find its low-key, private-house decor less appealing than the more raffish sawdust-floored Palm Too or the showbiz, speakeasy aura of Frankie and Johnnie's. Dining in the small, rather bare rooms of the house may not appeal to me, but the supreme quality of the meats and vegetables does. So it does also to the well-heeled customers who devour giant steaks and lobsters while they chat about cross-country flights and the market. A house favorite is the spinach salad. While not made to order, this is still one of the best in the city, the chilled wilted spinach leaves laden with chunks of meaty bacon. Waiters are non-assertive and protective—the kind who bring the peppermill before you ask. If you are alone in Manhattan and seek company, ask for a seat at the "traveler's table" when you make your reservation. This long bare table positioned just outside the teeming kitchen, in eye view of all traffic, would be Siberia elsewhere, but is the congenial "in" place here. Everything but the crusty hash browns is à la carte and there is no menu. Since you must order sight unseen, here are typical prices to guide you: salads $4.50; onion rings $3.95; vegetables $2.75; steaks $15.50; fish $10-$15; lobsters $25 up; coffee $1. Nothing spectacular on the wine list, but there is a lovely Meursault Charmes and some superior Chiantis. You'll pour your own wine in this busy place.

CHRIST CELLA, 160 East 46th Street, Manhattan. Telephone: (212) OX7-2479. Hours: 12-10:30, daily. Cards: AE, BA/Visa, CB, DC, MC. Reservations suggested. Street parking. Full bar service.

Manhattan: Greenwich Village
THE COACH HOUSE
American

$$$

New York is a little world by itself. You can find cuisines from African to Yugoslavian, sometimes without leaving your neighborhood. But rarest of all is—American. One of New York's most aristocratic restaurants, and a historic landmark besides, is The Coach House. (The ceiling still has a visible slot where once hay was pitched down to horses.) Owned by a fastidious gentleman of Greek descent, The Coach House sometimes lists moussaka, shish kebab, or the like, but the dishes it is famous for are American—Southern, if you are a purist. Start with black bean soup Madeira (almost a purée, with a few mashed beans for texture, laced with a slosh of fine liquor), and end with American pecan pie (absolutely the best of its kind, with a tissue-thin crust and a heavenly filling instead of the syrupy gum that often sabotages this national treasure). In between enjoy such delights as juicy roast turkey, roast prime ribs, chicken pie, fresh lump crabmeat with julienned ham, or a carpetbag steak (stuffed with oysters). Almost before you order your cocktail or overpriced wine, a waiter appears with hot cornsticks. From then on it's heady going. Fish, and the crabmeat Baltimore are as fresh as the stern-eyed master can pry from the markets. And steak *au poivre* is a fine strip of prime meat napped with a peppery brown glaze that is a world away from the soupy cream sauce that so often corrupts this dish.

THE COACH HOUSE, 110 Waverly Place, Manhattan. Telephone: (212) SP7-0303. Hours: 5:30-11, Tuesday-Sunday; closed Monday. Cards: AE, DC, MC. Reservations required. Street parking. Full bar service.

Dinner

Appetizer or Soup (Choice)

Fresh Mushrooms à la Grecque   Fresh Eggplant Provencale
Fresh Clams 1.50   Smoked Turkey
Quiche Lorraine   Paté Maison   Chilled Tomato Juice
Herring in Cream   Fresh Fruit
Escargots de Bourgogne Sauteed with Croutons in Garlic Butter (for two) 7.00
Fresh Melon -- Fresh Oysters 3.50

Soups

The Coach House Black Bean Soup Madeira
Soup of the Day

Entrees

Prime Ribs of Beef, Natural	22.00
Mignonettes of Veal a la Campagne with Glazed Chestnuts	22.85
Veal Piccate à la Francaise	20.50
(Medaillons of Milk-Fed Veal Sauteed in a Delicate Wine Sauce)	
Long Island Duckling - Brandied Quince	19.85
Fresh Oysters Coach House	22.85
Stuffed with Lump Crab Meat and Baked with Mornay Sauce.	
Fresh Lump Crabmeat Baltimore, Sauteed with Julienne Ham	22.50
Delightful Striped Bass Cooked in its Own Court Bouillon with Vegetables	22.50
Baby Lobster Tails Sauteed in Garlic Butter	22.00
Fresh Striped Bass vin Blanc	22.50
Baby Lobster Tails Skorpios with Feta Cheese	22.85

Vegetables and Potatoes

Baked Idaho Potato   Fresh Vegetable of the Day
Rice Pilaff   Potato of the Day

Choice of Fresh Vegetable, or
Fresh Garden Mixed Salad with Our Dressing

Desserts

(All Baking is done in our kitchen)

The Coach House Chocolate Cake   Dacquoise   Fresh Apple Tart
Coupe aux Marrons   Fresh Melon   Fresh Strawberries
Grand Marnier Bavarois   American Pecan Pie
Lemon Sherbet   Hot Fudge Ice Cream Cake
Chef's Custard   Ice Cream

Imported Cheeses

Coffee, Tea, Milk   Espresso Coffee .60 extra

Manhattan: Midtown West
COPENHAGEN
Danish $$

The Danes may be melancholy but they enjoy their food. At Copenhagen, the chefs blend their own house mustard, make their own sausages (or have them custom-made) and create a coffee blend that just might be the best in town. The oval room is striped with green drapes and tall mirrors. In the center a great round table groans under some 30 *koldt bord* offerings—there are 10 kinds of herring alone. About two-thirds of this table features cold delicacies; these are superior to the hot ones, which tend to suffer steam table-itis. Guests just keep going back with fresh plates to help themselves to cold dishes, then hot dishes, then fruits and sweets, and no one keeps count. While smorgasbording is fun, I prefer to sit at my table and order from the regular menu, after first observing the Danish ritual nip: akvavit poured from a bottle centered in a giant ice cube. Danish pumpernickel, mealy and nutty-tasting, is deliciously fresh. Dumpling soup contains two kinds of slippery little dumplings in a bowl of glistening gold chicken stock. Among main dishes many hearty items appeal, but most of all I enjoy the homemade sausages, non-greasy and in a zesty sauce, with sweet-hot Danish mustard on the side. Vegetables, particularly the red cabbage, are overcooked. The bottle that stands on most tables is crisp Carlsberg beer, but a moderately priced wine list includes some German wines that go nicely with this well-seasoned food. The Danish *koldt bord,* with dessert and coffee, is $13.75; the full menu is à la carte.

COPENHAGEN, 68 West 58th Street, Manhattan. Telephone: (212) 688-3690. Hours: 12-3, 5-11, Monday-Friday; 12-11, Saturday; closed Sunday. Cards: AE, CB, DC, MC. Reservations suggested. Parking in nearby garage. Full bar service.

EGGS & SPECIALTIES

"Københavner Omelet" Copenhagen Omelet, with Danish Shrimps and Mushrooms, Crisp Lettuce & Tomatoes.	6.75
Danish Cheese Omelet.	6.50
Omelet, with Finely Chopped Ham, Chives.	6.75
Omelet Confiture.	6.50
Prime Sirloin Steak, Grilled Tomatoes, Mushrooms, Fresh Crisp Salad.	13.00
English Boeuf, with Fried Egg and Smothered Onions.	13.00
"Hakkebof med Log og Spejlaeg" Prime Cut, Chopped Steak, with Onions and Fried Egg.	8.50
"Bøf a la Lindstrøm" Chopped Prime Beef, Mixed with Chopped Onions, Red Beets, Capers, Parsley Potatoes.	8.50
Steak Tartar, Scraped Filet of Prime Beef, Raw Egg Yolk, Chopped Onions, Red Beets, Capers, Anchovies, Fresh Horseradish.	9.00
Danish Style Pork Chops, Sautéed with Onions, Cucumber Salad.	8.50
Two Small Chopped Steaks in Brown Onion Sauce, Pickled Red Beets.	8.50
Danish Frikadeller, Red Cabbage, Sugar-Browned Potatoes.	7.75
"Hjemmelavet, Medisterpølse" Homemade Sausage, Red Cabbage, Sugar-Browned Potatoes.	7.75
"Biksemad med Spejlaeg" Danish Roast Beef Hash with Fried Egg.	7.75

Manhattan: Upper East Side
CORIANDER
Exotic $$

During its birth pangs, Coriander strove to be a Thai restaurant, but something Italian got in the way. Today, do not expect to find authentic Asian dishes. Rather think of Coriander as a chummy neighborhood spot where you can order chicken and fish with an enigmatic tinge of ginger and soy. Or a lovely dish of cared-about pasta. I find most of the Oriental sauces a tiny bit too sweet for my taste; and certainly no restaurant in Thailand would serve a hot peanut sauce as mild. If you are not overly adventurous however, and do like a hint of the unusual, the menu at Coriander will please you. Entering past the cozy length of bar, you have a choice of the rear room with a view of the tiny kitchen or the front near the glowing open fireplace. The artichoke vinaigrette is delicious; with the homemade mayonnaise verte it is even better. But the standout among the appetizers is a warm sliced country sausage accompanied with a sauce redolent of Chinese hoisin. Or you might split one of the pastas, for two or even four. Chicken *gai*

Hickory Smoked Spareribs
with Specially Blended Sauce 7.95

Roast Boneless Duckling a la Maison 8.95

Mussels
with Lime Sauce 6.95

Sauteed Herbed Shrimp
with Lemon Parslied Butter 8.95

Gai Pud Nor Mai
Chicken with Baby Corn and Straw Mushrooms 7.50

Gai Pud Khing
Chicken with Fresh Ginger, Black Mushrooms and Scallions 7.25

Filet of Sole a la Maison 7.25

yang is a typical Coriander original: half a marinated chicken in an Oriental sweet and sour sauce, perched on top of "Coriander potatoes," a sort of hash brown, piquant with green pepper, and mysteriously flavored with a soylike seasoning. The highlight here, though, is *gai pud khing,* a lively serving of skinless chicken white meat nuggets aswim in a sauce perky with fresh ginger, scallions and what the house calls black mushrooms, but which are really another fungus, "tree ears." Desserts also have an original touch. Chocolate sour cream pie is a pale thing, not a must for true chocolate lovers, but light and delicate. Key lime cheese pie is a glossy sensation. The pecan pie is commercial but a quite good version. Coffee is also good, and espressos come with anisette on the house. À la carte main dishes range from $6.50 to $9. The small wine list provides satisfying wines at a decent price.

CORIANDER, 314 East 72nd Street, Manhattan. Telephone: (212) 794-2700. Hours: 6-12, daily. Cards: AE, DC. Reservations advised. Parking in nearby garage. Full bar service.

Chicken Gai Yang
　Half Marinated Chicken with Hot and Sweet Sauce 6.95

Thailand Beef Salade
　Sauteed Chopped Beef with Hot Pepper, Red Onion and Scallions 6.95

Zuppa de Vongole
　with Pasta Seasoned with Garlic and Cheese 8.95

Fettucine Alfredo 5.95

Fettucine Carbonara 6.25

Calamari
　Deep Batter Fried Fresh Squid 5.95

Prime Sliced Steak Sandwich
　Served with Spinach Salad and Garlic Bread 7.95

Manhattan: Midtown West
CREPE SUZETTE
French
$

Don't ask how they wrap a lamb chop in a crêpe at Crêpe Suzette. They don't. The name came long before the current roll-it-in-a-crêpe craze. This is a restaurant of contrasts: Some dishes miss, while others make you want to become a steady customer. The wine list mentions no labels, shippers or vintages, yet it presents over 30 wines, and the most expensive is a modest $10. Another paradox: While it looks like a cozy bistro, Crêpe Suzette is geared to the theater crowd. Waiters have no time to chat; they are deadly serious in getting your food on the table so you can make curtain time. Still, they are so efficient you will never get the feeling of being rushed. After the shows begin, the pace slows and no one cares how long you stay. A filet mignon Stroganoff (a Tuesday night special) is a generous plate of tender filet morsels with a good creamy sauce and a mound of rice that is exemplary for a French restaurant. Double lamb chops are so tender you scarcely need a knife. Beef Wellington is only $7.50, and a high peak is reached at $9.50 for a steak *au poivre*. Every meat I've tried has been equal to that served in French restaurants charging twice the price. Wine is also available at prices that make you feel you are getting two for one. A Graves from the House of Burgundy is $5. Taittinger Champagne is $14. The most expensive red is a B&G Pommard '74 at just $10. Many people are unaware that this strange little place exists, handy to theaters on restaurant row. Alas, for them.

CRÊPE SUZETTE, 313 West 46th Street, Manhattan. Telephone: (212) 974-9002, 581-9719. Hours: 12-3, 4-10, Monday-Friday; 4-11, Saturday; closed Sunday. No credit cards. Reservations suggested. Parking in nearby lots. Full bar service.

Les Poissons

Crepes Seafood 5.00
Brook trout meuniere 5.50
Shrimps Scampy 7.50
Scallops Sauté Provençale 5.50
English Sole amandine (for 2) 15.00
Frogs legs Provençale 6.00

Entrées

Canard à l'orange 7.00
Veal Scallopini Normande 6.50
Veal Kidney sauté Bordelaise 5.00
Sweet Breads sauté Financiere 6.50
Coq au Vin 4.50
Boeuf Bourguignon 5.00
Broiled double Lamb chops 8.50
Broiled sirloin steak 8.50
Steak au poivre 9.50
Broiled Filet Mignon 9.50
Chateaubriant (for 2) 25.00
Roast Rack of Lamb (for 2) 25.00
Broiled double Sirloin Steak (for 2) 25.00
Filet Mignon Wellington 7.50

Manhattan: Upper East Side
CZECHOSLOVAK PRAHA
Czechoslovakian $

In Czechoslovakia *knedlicky* (bread dumplings) are so omnipresent that they even make jokes about their leadenness in sci-fi films there. At New York's Praha the dumplings are light and spongy, just right for soaking up the hearty gravies and sauces that accompany the somewhat monochromatic fare of the Czechs. What stands out here are the crackling, brown-skinned and totally fat-free duckling; and the jumbo portions of rich roast goose, the latter at $10.50, more expensive than even broiled filet mignon with mushrooms ($9.75). These prices are for a full dinner, including soup, entrée, two vegetables, dessert and beverage. That super duckling and another specialty, rabbit in cream sauce, are only $7.75. There are 30 *table d'hôte* meals under $8.50 to choose from, so you need not fear for your pocketbook when you dine at Praha. A must is the *palacinky* (traditional large Czech crêpes). These are included on the dinner and may be rolled either with apricot jam or *lekvar,* prune jam. There are moderately priced wines from Hungary and Germany that go well with the hearty food, but better still is the good Urquell Pilsner, with 100-proof slivovitz to start off the feast.

CZECHOSLOVAK PRAHA, 1358 First Avenue, Manhattan. Telephone: (212) 988-3505. Hours: 12-11, daily. Cards: AE. Reservations suggested. Parking in nearby garage. Full bar service.

Soups

Beef Consomme (Hovezi Polevka)   Soup Du Jour
DINNER INCLUDES: TOMATO JUICE, SOUP, OR FRUIT COCKTAIL,

ENTREE: 2 Vegetables or 1 Vegetable and 1 Salad
Dessert and Beverage   A La Carte .50 less

Entrees

ROAST GOOSE (Pecena Husa)	10.50
ROAST LONG ISLAND DUCKLING (Pecena Kachna)	7.75
ROAST LOIN OF PORK (Veprova Pecene)	8.25
RABBITS IN CREAM SAUCE (Zajic na Smetane)	7.75
BEEF WITH CREAM SAUCE (Svickova)	7.75
BOILED BEEF WITH DILL SAUCE (Hovezi Koprova)	7.75
BEEF STROGANOFF	7.75
STUFFED CABBAGE (Plnene Zeli)	7.00
SERBIAN GOULASH, (Srbsky Gulas)	7.75
BEEF GOULASH (Hovezi Gulas)	7.50
SZEGEDIN GOULASH (Szegedinsky Gulas)	7.25
ROAST CHICKEN ½ BROILER (Pecene Kure)	7.50
SOUTHERN FRIED CHICKEN (Smazene Kure)	7.75
CHICKEN LIVER BUDAPEST	7.75
SHISH KE BAB (Raznici)	8.25
CZECHOSLOVAK SAUSAGE PLATTER (Klobasa-Debrecinka-Jirtnice	7.50
CALVES BRAINS WITH EGGS (Mozecek s Veici)	6.75
BREADED CALVES BRAINS (Smazeny teleci mozecek)	7.50
VEAL CUTLET NATURAL (Prirodni teleci rizek)	8.25
VEAL CUTLET CORDON BLEU (Plneny teleci rizek)	8.75
WIENER SCHNITZEL (Smazený teleci rizek)	8.25
VEAL SCHNITZEL "PARIS" (Teleci Parizky rizek)	8.25
VEAL SCHNITZEL A LA HOLSTEIN (Holstinsky rizek)	8.50
DUMPLINGS WITH EGGS (Knedlicky s veici)	6.00
BREADED MUSHROOMS (Smazene Zampiony)	6.75
FRUIT DUMPLINGS (Ovocne Kendlicky)	7.25

Sea Food

FILET OF SOLE	7.50
HALIBUT STEAK	7.50
FILET OF FLOUNDER	7.50
SHRIMP	8.00
SCALLOPS	8.00

Manhattan: Upper East Side
DAVID K'S CHUNG KUO YUAN
Chinese
$$

Some object to a Chinese establishment that charges as much as a good French restaurant. Yet why not? This is no formica-top, paper-napkin noodle joint. David K's is a lovely dining place with a wall-long window looking onto a patio. Waiters wear tuxedoes, crystal is Rosenthal and linens are virginal. Here a waiter will spring across the room to refill your wine glass or light your lady's cigarette. Chung Kuo Yuan, which translates Chinese Garden, is an *haute cuisine* temple of gastronomy, with food, service and ambience equal to that of a magnificent French or Italian restaurant. Such trappings, such attentive service cannot come cheap. The food is prepared by four superb chefs and most of it looks as beautiful as a bouquet. *Dim sum,* little steam cakes, are feather-light and dainty. Peking duck is gorgeous in presentation, although expensive at $26. Oyster beef is far from ordinary, served elegantly on a bed of fresh asparagus tips and dotted with glossy black mushrooms. Instead of the familiar *mo shu* pork, David K's serves venison in see-through thin pancakes. There is even a delicate dessert, *tan t'a,* a tiny tart filled with a semi-sweet lemon custard, bedded in a short-crust pastry. David Keh is a restaurateur of long experience and his is a splendid representation of a splendid cuisine. Luncheons will cost about $8; at dinner à la carte items vary, but a complete meal will be $15 upward. Chinese banquets are available at $35 per person for a table of 10.

DAVID K'S CHUNG KUO YUAN, 1117 Third Avenue, Manhattan. Telephone: (212) 371-9090. Hours: 12-3, 7-12, Sunday-Thursday; until 12:30 Friday-Saturday. Cards: AE. Reservations suggested. Street parking. Full bar service.

海鮮類　　　　　　　*Seafood*

干燒明蝦	Jumbo shrimp, Szechuen style	9.50
紅燒明蝦	Prawns in brown sauce	8.75
干煎蝦碌	Pan fried shrimp in shell	8.75
芙蓉蝦片	Velvet shrimp	8.75
魚香蝦片	Sliced shrimp with garlic sauce	8.75
干燒田鷄	Frog's legs, Szechuen style	9.50
魚香干貝	Scallops with garlic sauce	8.75
清炒干貝	Sauteed scallops	8.75
椒鹽鯧魚	Pomfort fish with pepper/salt	12.00
糟溜魚片	Sliced fish with wine sauce	8.75
松子魚	Catch of the day in a sweet & sour sauce	9.50
清蒸魚	Steamed fish	12.00
溜青蟹	Crab with brown sauce	9.50
干燒龍蝦球	Lobster, Szechuen style	15.00
魚香龍蝦	Fresh lobster with garlic sauce	19.50
碧綠龍蝦	Fresh lobster sauteed with fresh vegetables	19.50

Manhattan: Midtown East
DIVAN TURKISH CUISINE
Turkish $$

Few places where a complete meal averages just a little over $10 can match Divan for quality of food, service and atmosphere. Unlike many Middle Eastern establishments, food here is delicate, pretty on the plate and most carefully prepared. In Turkey a divan is a room set aside for drinking and smoking; the ambience at Divan is more like a Victorian dining room. The little table lamps and red velvet drapes are more 1890s than Seljuk. There are, however, some splendid blow-ups of old Turkish engravings that depict scenes along the Golden Horn, and Turkish songs moan sweetly in the background. Divan claims its chef has written a three-volume work on Turkish cooking. His skill shows. Soups are superlative, my favorite being a mushroom-yoghurt that is actually a suave cream of chicken with mushroom flecks, made gloriously tasty by a dash of yoghurt. Main dishes are above reproach: A Stendahl Choice is lamb on a bed of puréed eggplant—divine at Divan. Another lovely dish is filet of flounder stuffed with crabmeat. With most entrées comes a delicately buttered pilaf and a crisp salad with a gently herbed cream dressing. Desserts, if you have the room, are delicate and honey-sweet. Both American and Turkish coffee are good. Disappointing is the fact that they have no Turkish wines, but the small choice available is well priced with some in the $7 to $9 range. Luncheons are about $4.50; complete dinners chosen from the à la carte menu will run $10 and upward.

DIVAN TURKISH CUISINE, 338 East 49th Street, Manhattan. Telephone: (212) 826-1044. Hours: 12-3, 5:30-11, Monday-Friday; 5-11, Saturday-Sunday. Cards: AE, BA/Visa, CB, DC, MC. Reservations suggested. Parking in nearby garage. Full bar service.

Sidewalk vegetable stands, Mulberry Street, 1892.

Manhattan: Midtown East
EAMONN DORAN
Irish Pub

$$

True pubs are still unknown to New York, their gentle ways apparently being foreign to the bustling American nature. At this interesting new place, there is a pseudo-publike saloon upfront—a watering hole for young singles and doubles who like hustle music and loud conversations. In the rear is a modest dining room, innocent of any decor, with roomy booths for serious diners. Eamonn Doran himself runs this enterprising dream and seems determined to uphold his family's tradition of 200 years of pub-owning on the "ould sod." Not a holiday goes by without some kind of special celebration menu—Easter, Thanksgiving, Christmas, New Year's, Valentine's Day—if it is on the calendar, Eamonn has a menu for it. Doran has a special sherry "stop" daily, where in cocktail hours you can sample top-flight sherries and munch *tapas*, appetizing tidbits such as scallops in bacon, cold duck salad or sherry trifle. There is also a champagne and sangría brunch with Irish-accented dishes, including smoked Irish salmon. Regular menus are in both Gaelic and English, and there are some intriguing Irish specials, such as a tasty steak and kidney pie and *Gaeltacht* chicken, a roast chicken with ham and a spiced dressing. Caesar salad is quite authentic, and among the desserts is a rather staggering mélange of fruits, cake and liquor modestly called Irish sherry trifle. Hearty lunches run from $3 to $8; substantial dinners range between $7 and $15.

EAMONN DORAN, 998 Second Avenue, Manhattan. Telephone: (212) 753-9191, 752-8088. Hours: 11 am-4 am, daily. Cards: AE, BA/Visa, DC. Reservations suggested. Parking in nearby garage. Full bar service.

Entrées

Gaeltacht Chicken—Ireland   7.95
Roast Chicken with Ham and Stuffing, Baked Potato

Steak and Kidney Pie— United Kingdom   6.95
A beautiful Beef and Kidney Dish. Baked m its own Pastry

Veal Picata—Italy   8.95
Italian Classic served with Shoestring Potatoes

Veal Normande—Normandy   8.95
Calvados Cream Sauce, served with Rice Pilaf

Rack of Lamb—Australia   14.95
Tender Succulent Lamb, Roasted to your liking (Per Person) with a Garden of Vegetables

Entrecôte au Poivre Vert—Paris   12.95
Green Peppercorn Steak, flambeed with Cognac and served with Shoestring Potatoes

Tournedos Bordelaise—Bordeaux   10.95
Fillet with a Marrow Bone and Red Wine Sauce served with Rice Pilaf

Caneton À L'Orange—France   8.95
Roast Crisp Duckling served on a bed of Wild Rice

Steak Teriyaki—Japan   10.95
Prime Steak marinated in our original recipe and served with a Baked Potato

Medaillons de Porc Aux Pruneaux—Brittany   7.95
Light cream Sorrel Sauce

Manhattan: Greenwich Village and Upper West Side
EL FARO
Spanish $

El Faro was a gustatorial lighthouse in a dreary section of lower Manhattan long before many of its present customers were born. In early days its policy of no reservations created long lines outside, patiently waiting for tables to be released by diners who enjoyed lingering over hearty food, and conversations that seemed at times to include everyone in the place. Habitués often came in the afternoon, brought a book, and sat hours at the bar reading, sipping margaritas and whetting their thirst with salty Serrano ham and black olives. Customers ranged then and still do from butchers in blood-stained aprons from the nearby wholesale meat district to chattering young groups in jeans to uptowners in evening dress. Food is inexpensive, robust; the metal casseroles and china platters come heaped high. The paellas are among the best, and the various seafoods in green sauce are always popular. The Stendahl Choice goes to chicken Villarroy, two large boneless chicken breasts with béchamel cream sealed under a breading, rather like a peasant version

Shrimp a la Faro (Broiled with Wine Sauce)	6.25
Paella a la Valenciana (Rice, Chicken, Sausages, Clams, Scallops and Shrimps)	7.00
Paella a la Valenciana with Lobster	9.00
Paella a la Marinera (Rice, Clams, Scallops and Shrimps)	7.00
Paella a la Marinera with Lobster	9.00
Mariscada with Egg Sauce (Mixed Seafood)	7.00
Mariscada al Ajillo (Hot Sauce with Garlic)	7.00
Mariscada with Green Sauce, Olive Oil, Parsley, Garlic, Onions)	7.00
Crab-Meat with Green Sauce	8.50
Lobster with White Sauce (Sherry Wine, Butter, Milk and Onions)	8.50
Lobster with Green Sauce	8.50
Shrimp a la Diablo (Hot Sauce, Onions, Green Peppers and Tomatoes)	6.25

of chicken Kiev. Another fortifying splendor is *veal à la extremeña,* a plate that overflows with veal, onions and peppers, accompanied with a mountain of good dry yellow rice spiked with spicy chorizo sausage. Every entrée comes with a house salad. The sweet-hot tomatoey house dressing is famous. There is a respectable choice of Spanish wines at easy prices, but what you see on most tables are huge pitchers of sangría, or simply beer in quantity. At times I also enjoy Quarante-y-Tres (Licor 43) a most unusual Spanish liqueur that seems to combine many different tastes in one glass.

El Faro 72 is a sister restaurant on the upper West Side. Food and prices are almost identical, but service is a bit more formal. 72 also takes credit cards, and permits reservations, which makes it handy for patrons of Lincoln Center.

EL FARO, 823 Greenwich Street, Manhattan. Telephone: (212) WA9-8210. 10 am-midnight, daily. No credit cards. Reservations not accepted. Street parking. Full bar service. EL FARO 72, 40 West 72nd Street. Telephone: (212) EN 2-2050. Cards: AE, BA/Visa, CB, DC, MC. Reservations accepted.

```
Shrimp with Green Sauce .................................6.25
Shrimp a la Criolla .......................................6.25
Shrimp and Rice (Shrimp cooked with Saffron Rice) .......6.25
Shrimp al Ajillo (Hot Sauce with Garlic) .................6.25
Beef Saute (Oregano, Bay Leaves and Wine) .............6.25
Filet of Pork Bar B. Q. with Almond Sauce ...............6.25
Spare Ribs with Bar B. Q. with Fruit Sauce ..............6.50
Clams a la Marinera (Olive Oil, Parsley, Garlic,
    Onions and Oregano) ................................6.25
Clams a la Burdalesa (Hot Sauce) .......................6.25
Cornish Hen a la Espanola (Wine, Onions, Bay Leaves
    and Clove) .........................................6.50
```
All Dishes are served with Spanish Rice or Spanish Potatoes and Salad.

Manhattan: Midtown East
EL PARADOR
Mexican
$

El Parador is probably the best Mexican restaurant in New York, yet it is almost impossible to get a meal here. Not just because it is always crowded, but also because it is usually impossible to find a parking place, and because of the house policy of no reservations and stay-at-the-bar-and-drink-till-we-call-you. The only way to enter this *corrida* is to grab the bull by the horns of its dilemma: Come thirsty, count on a long wait at the overcrowded bar, and expect to spend as much for drinks as for food. (Some of those clinging to their bar stools as if they were life rafts never seem to get a table, but I presume that is by choice.) Once you are settled amid white-washed Mexican surroundings, the food proves to be worth the wait. El Parador understands the simple majesty of Mexican cooking—the proper cheese, good thick sauces, fresh tortillas, decently prepared rice and beans and the imperative of blistering hot plates. If you like your guacamole garlicky, this is the place. All the familiar combination plates are here, but they are prettier to look at and taste better than in most New York haciendas. With the rice and beans on the side, these are substantial meals at $6.75. Unique to this establishment is *huevos a la Tampiquena,* scrambled eggs with onions, tomatoes, chorizo sausage, and chiles, plus a cheese enchilada, salad, rice and beans—all for $6. There is also the house special chicken, *pollo Parador,* at $7.50, a delicious marinated chicken steamed with onions and garlic. The Mexican and Philippine beers are good.

EL PARADOR, 325 East 34th Street, Manhattan. Telephone: (212) 679-6812. Hours: 5-11, Monday-Saturday; closed Sunday. No credit cards. Reservations not accepted. Street parking. Full bar service.

CARNES

SHREDDED SPICED BEEF 6.50
   Sauteed in a spicy mole sauce with
   fried green bananas, rice and beans
PICADILLO A LA CRIOLLA 6.50
   Chopped meat, creole style,
   mild fried green bananas, rice and beans
CHILE CON CARNE 5.50
   Served with chopped onions,
   Jalapano sauce, rice and salad

MARISCOS

CAMARONES MALAGUENA 7.50
   Shrimp in a butter, wine and
   almond sauce; rice, beans, salad

CAMARONES TORRES 7.50
   Shrimp fried in an egg batter,
   lemon wedges, rice, beans, salad

CAMARONES PIQUANT 7.50
   Shrimp in a spicy sauce, rice, beans, salad

CAMARONES EN SALSA VERDE. 7.50
   Fresh shrimps in a green
   parsley wine and garlic sauce served
   on a bed of Spanish saffron rice

POLLOS 30 minutes plus

POLLO EN MOLE 7.50
   Chicken in a piquant mole sauce, rice
POLLO EN MOLE VERDE 7.50
   Chicken simmered in a green
   tomatillo sauce
POLLO PARADOR 7.50
   Marinated chicken, steamed with
   onions and garlic

Manhattan: Midtown East
FLOWER DRUM
Chinese
$$

Chinese restaurants of quality in midtown are scarcer than dragon's teeth. A reliably good one is Flower Drum. It's near the United Nations, where the owner began his cooking career, and many of his former customers are among the regulars. Flower Drum's uniqueness lies in its seasonally changing menu. Entering past a generally buzzing bar, one is seated amid a fantasy of Taiwanese decor: dragons of gilt and firecracker red, backlighted screens and silken lanterns. There is a little open-sided teahouse with just enough table space for a pair of lovers. Among spring selections is chicken jade, white meat of chicken combined with fresh asparagus. Summer brings lichee delight, *fresh* lichees with chicken, pineapple and loquats served in a hollowed pineapple shell. Another traditional summer food is squab in a jade nest, minced squab sautéed with fresh water chestnuts, bamboo shoots, Chinese mushrooms and green peas, served wrapped in a crisp lettuce leaf. In autumn, crab imperial is featured, combining fresh crabs and a garlic-ginger sauce with wine and scallions. In winter, *hoa gow*, the bronze firepot, is set at tableside with a compartment of bubbling broth. Each guest selects chicken, fish, beef, lamb and cellophane noodles to dip at will. At the end, the flavored broth is served as a scented soup. Typical house dinners are $5.75, but the specials are apt to run from $6.50 to $8 each, depending on their complexity.

FLOWER DRUM, 856 Second Avenue, Manhattan. Telephone: (212) 697-4280. Hours: 11:30-11, Monday-Thursday; until midnight, Friday-Saturday; noon-11, Sunday. Cards: AE, BA/Visa, CB, DC, MC. Reservations suggested. Parking in nearby garage. Full bar service.

Fulton Market, 1868.

Manhattan: Midtown East
THE FOUR SEASONS
Continental $$$

This is one of the world's great restaurants. A few find The Four Seasons austere, and some expense-account diners underrate the kitchen. I suspect it is because they order grilled steaks and potatoes, which are fine but not extraordinary. What is extraordinary are the fabulous sauces that transform most entrées into achievements. And I know of no other New York restaurant that shows such continuing imagination in devising unusual food combinations, and in the serving of vegetables not to be found on other menus. To sit beneath the vast ceiling beside the murmuring pool, watching the great metal chain curtains rippling magically against the tremendous glass walls always stirs me into anticipation of a dining experience, rather than a mere meal. The spaciousness of the tables, the eagle-eyed captains and solicitous waiters, the vast wine list, and oh, those sauces, and those desserts, have always more than fulfilled my expectations. One can spend a fortune exploring the wine list (over 50 American wines alone), but one can also discover bargains and little-known wines as well. One orders fish or duckling or veal here with full assurance that it will be the best and freshest of its kind, prepared by a master chef. It seems to be that there are not as many delightful seasonal changes in the menu as previously, but that is a quibble compared to what one can order in this temple of gastronomy.

Among appetizers are goose rillette, small clams with green onions and truffles, and oysters with horseradish and ginger. Or you can have baked clams with almonds and herbs, or calf's brains in herb-mustard crumbs. A winter cream of vegetable soup tastes daringly of turnip, a spring vegetable is as fresh as flowers. Striped bass on fennel with Pernod (for two) is handsomely flambéed tableside. *Plume de veau* with crabmeat and mushrooms is a heady delight. Winter also brings items such as wild boar with gorgonzola polenta. Two roast quails with sage and fried grapes is another deft innovation. Some of the interesting vegetables I have savored are magnificent potatoes *rösti* (Renggli, the chef, is Swiss), nutted wild rice, and—an absolute stunner—baked fennel with Parmesan (finocchio simmered in rich chicken broth, topped with cheese and glazed under the broiler). This is the only American restaurant where I've seen fiddlehead ferns on the menu. Desserts range from individual soufflés done in coffee cups to wonders stacked high on a giant trolley. There is nothing in the world quite like the "fancy cake," a chocolate wonder, but every sweet is a high-caloric masterpiece. Entrées begin at $12.50. There is an outrageous $2.75 cover charge at dinner.

THE FOUR SEASONS, 99 East 52nd Street, Manhattan. Telephone: (212) PL4-9494. Hours: 12-3, 5-11:30, Monday-Saturday; closed Sunday. Cards: AE, BA/Visa, CB, DC, MC. Reservations required. Valet parking after 6. Full bar service.

Sea and Fresh Water Fish

The Four Seasons LOBSTER Soufflé (30 minutes) 18.50
STRIPED BASS FOR TWO: Flamed on Fennel with Pernod 26.50
... or Poached in White Wine and Herbs 24.50
The Classic TRUITE AU BLEU 11.50
❀ A Ragout of SHRIMPS and SCALLOPS, Lobster Sauce 15.50

This Evening's Entrées

Filet of PLUME DE VEAU with CRAB MEAT and MUSHROOMS 16.50
❀ Steamed CALF'S LIVER with Mushrooms and Shallots 12.50
Escalope of VEAL sautéed in Lemon Butter 14.50

Steaks, Chops and Birds

BROILED OVER CHARCOAL
CALF'S LIVER — Thick, Sage Butter 12.50
SIRLOIN STEAK or FILET MIGNON 15.00
Twin Double LAMB Chops 15.50
Skillet STEAK with Smothered Onions 16.50
❀ Two Roast QUAILS with Sage and Fried Grapes 14.50

Manhattan: Midtown West
FRANKIE AND JOHNNIE'S
Steakhouse $$

The Times Square area is a difficult one in which to find good food. Frankie and Johnnie's has been winning friends and influencing palates ever since it was a speakeasy in 1926. Don't expect ambience—expect top quality steaks. On the street there is only a small sign and a doorway. Up some creaky stairs and into the restaurant, you find a kitchen that would seem more appropriate to a neighborhood diner, a brightly lighted dining room unmolested by decor except for a few theatrical posters on the walls—and Max, the host. On your first visit, Max is apt to plunk himself down at your table to talk about the theater, his steaks, or your choice. On your second visit, Max is sure to plunk himself at your table. That's how friendships are made at this purely American steakhouse. Broadway celebrities may be adjacent. Don't accost them; they are deep into a large slab of perfectly done, first-rate beef. I agree

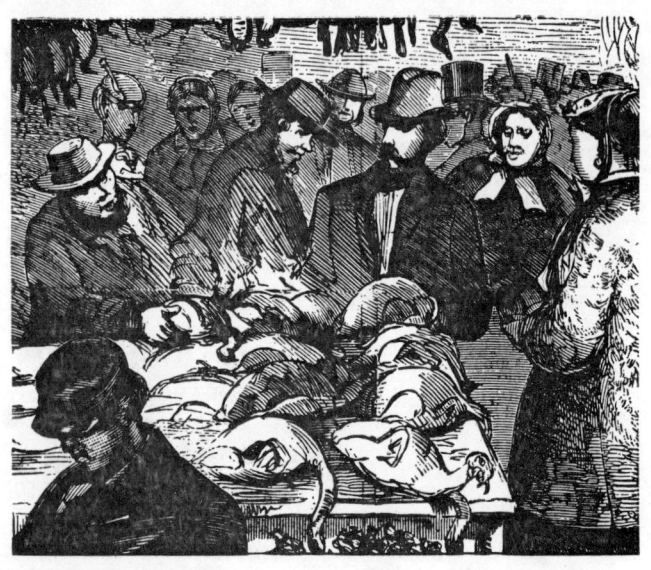

Fulton Market, 1868

with Max when he says there are two kinds of steakhouses: One serves a football of steak, plump and red in the center, charred on the outside; the second serves a steak that is larger, a bit thinner, with the bone in. Frankie and Johnnie's is of the latter variety. All meats are cooked over intensely high heat, then cut from the bone in big chunks at tableside just moments before serving. Max maintains that this keeps all juices sealed in till the last second. The onion rings are among the best in the city, and the house salad is almost a meal in itself. Few steakhouses—even at higher prices—can top the sirloin (12.50), the filet mignon ($13.50), or the beautiful double lamb chops ($12). Forget desserts, and the coffee is mediocre. There are a few ordinary wines around $9, but I recommend a bottle or two of Heineken or Lowenbrau.

FRANKIE AND JOHNNIE'S, 269 West 45th Street, Manhattan. Telephone: (212) 245-9717. Hours: 4:30-12:30, Monday-Saturday; closed Sunday. Cards: AE, BA/Visa, CB, DC, MC. Reservations suggested. Parking in nearby garage. Full bar service.

Manhattan: Midtown East
GAYLORD
Indian $$

Pukka Sahib and man your chukkers. There are Indian restaurants and Indian restaurants, and Gaylord is the most British. Muzak of soft pop instead of subtle sitar? We cater to the Western taste, murmurs the captain. Food, likewise. While an old India hand might find a meal here pleasant, interesting and appetizing, he will miss the sting of genuine Indian cooking. The more timid will welcome a chance to taste exotic dishes with no fear that even a vindaloo (traditionally the fiery furnace of Indian treats) will leave his lips with more than a tingle. Gaylord was first in New York with tandoori cooking—using a giant clay oven, stoked to blistering heat with charcoal, that can broil a chicken in 10 minutes and bake a *nan* (Indian leavened bread) in a minute or two. Anywhere you sit in Gaylord is blissful, for, despite its British leanings, this is one of the most suave and elegant of Indian restaurants. Lighting is romantic and the dining areas are all surrounded by suavity and art. Yet I prefer the

SIFARISH-E-KHAS

SPECIAL TANDOORI MIX   9.50
Tandoori chicken, Boti kebab, Sheekh Kebab, Chicken Tikka, Tandoori Prawn and Lamb Pasanda, Nukti Biryani (Rice fragrantly flavoured with saffron) Mixed vegetable or Dal, Onion Kulcha

SPECIAL 4 COURSE DINNER   8.50
Soup, Tandoori chicken *or* Chicken Pakora, Sheekh Kebab, Rogan Josh, Nan, Vegetable pullao, Dal special

SPECIAL VEGETARIAN THALI   7.50
Three varieties of Vegetables (Mattar Paneer, Aloo Gobi and Dal), Samosa, Pullao, Dahi Raita, Purees, Papadum and Dessert

rear room for its view of the tandoor ovens and its lovely murals that glow behind beaded curtains. *Shurat* (appetizers) are a must: The assorted platter is enough for two, and includes delicate *samosas* and *pakoras* (deep-fried fritters), a sampling of the chicken *tikka* (boneless cubes charcoaly from the tandoor), and—to my mind the best item in the house—the sheekh kebab, a cumin-spiced sausage made of minced lamb, onions and herbs and blistered in the tandoor. Entrées begin around $6. Lamb *vindaloo* isn't hot enough for me, and lamb *pasanda* is tastier elsewhere. Prawn *chilli masala* is slightly tingly and the prawns are fat and juicy. Perhaps best is the special tandoor mix, which offers little helpings of almost everything on the menu. There is a modest wine list, but beer is best.

GAYLORD (INDIA), 50 East 58th Street. Manhattan. Telephone: (212) 759-1710. Hours: 11:30-3, 5:30-11, Monday-Friday; 5:30-11, Saturday and Sunday. Cards: AE, BA/Visa, CB, DC, MC. Reservations required at dinner. Parking lot (150 E. 58th Street). Full bar service.

TANDOOR

TANDOORI CHICKEN   Full   7.25
                                      Half   4.50
Chicken marinated in yoghurt and mild spices, and cooked on charcoal in a clay oven

CHICKEN TIKKA   6.25
Boneless chicken pieces marinated and roasted Tandoori style

SHEEKH KEBAB   6.25
Minced lamb mixed with onions and herbs and roasted on skewers

FISH TIKKA KEBAB   6.25
Fish pieces marinated delicately and roasted Tandoori Style

Manhattan: Midtown West
GEORGES REY
French $

This impressive establishment has the air of a bigtime French restaurant of the fifties—and, amazingly, prices almost to match. There is a great deal of hubbub at lunchtime, when customers do not receive all the attention they deserve. In the quieter evenings you can better appreciate the charm of the place, as well as its food. Avoid the cramped tables in the bar. The main dining room is an ample squarish room, lowlit with a warm radiance. Every wall is covered with huge murals depicting scenes of Paris; psuedo-streetlamps heighten the nostalgic effect. Both luncheon and dinner menus feature *table d'hôte* meals of appetizer or soup, entrée, dessert and coffee. One mark of the quality here is that the uncommon soup *billi bi* is offered occasionally as *le potage du jour*, whereas many restaurants charge extra for this mussel-based cream soup. The kitchen seems particularly adroit with seafoods. Sole *amandine* is a large serving of tender filet, glistening gold, with lots of almonds. *La brochette de poulet à l'estragon* is a nice skewer of boneless chicken chunks that have been marinated with onions and peppers, served with a tarragon sauce. Desserts are made on the premises and are excellent, except for a miserable mousse. There is a modestly priced, moderately sized list of French wines, and some quite good French labels are offered as "house wines" at only $6.25 a bottle. Lunch will average about $8.75; complete dinners begin at only $8.75.

GEORGES REY, 60 West 55th Street, Manhattan. Telephone: (212) 245-6764. Hours: 12-11, Monday-Friday; 5-11, Saturday-Sunday. Cards: AE, BA/Visa, MC. Reservations suggested. Parking in nearby garage. Full bar service.

Entrees

OMELETTE AUX FRUITS DE MER 8.50
Seafood Omelette

LE FILET DE SOLE SAUTE BEURRE CITRON ou *Grillé* 9.75
Filet of Sole Butter, Lemon — or Broiled

FILET DE SOLE VERONIQUE 10.50
Filet of Sole Veronique

LA TRUITE DE RIVIERE AMANDINE 9.75
Fresh River Trout

LES QUENELLES DE BROCHET, GRATINEES 9.50
Mousse of Pike Fish, au Gratin

LES CUISSES DE GRENOUILLES PROVENCALE 10.75
Frog's Legs, Garlic, Tomatoes, Butter

LA SOLE ANGLAISE MEUNIERE OU GRILLEE 12.50
Imported Sole

LE BOUQUET DE CREVETTES ROSES, COTE D'AZUR 12.50
Shrimps, Scampi, Garlic, Tomatoes

LE POUSSIN AUX RAISINS 11.00
Fresh Whole Roast Baby Chicken, Grapes, Wine

LA BROCHETTE DE POULET A L'ESTRAGON 10.50
Boneless Country Fresh Chicken on a Skewer, Tarragon

LA POITRINE DE POULET CORDON BLEU 10.75
Boneless Breast of Chicken, Ham and Cheese

LE CANARD AUX CERISES 12.50
Duck, Cherries, Grand Marnier Sauce

FOIES DE VOLAILLE SAUTES BERCY 9.75
Chicken Livers, Sauteed Wine Shallots

LE FOIE DE VEAU A LA LYONNAISE 11.50
Calf's Liver, Sauteed Onions

ESCALOPE DE VEAU MEUNIERE 12.00
Escalope of Veal, Butter Lemon

L'ESCALOPE DE VEAU VILLEROY 12.50
Escalope of Veal, Mushroom Puree, Hollandaise

LE RIS DE VEAU BRAISE A l'ORANGE 12.75
Sweetbreads

LE FILET DE BOEUF PERIGOURDINE 12.75
Filet Mignon, Truffles Sauce

LE RUMPSTEAK AU POIVRE A L'ARMAGNAC 12.00
Pepper Steak

L'ENTRECOTE POELEE A L'ECHALOTE 12.75
Sirloin Steak, Sauteed Shallots

LES COTES D'AGNEAU VERT PRE 12.75
Broiled Lamb Chops

LE CARRE D'AGNEAU PERSILLE .... (Per Person) 12.75
Rack of Lamb au Jus

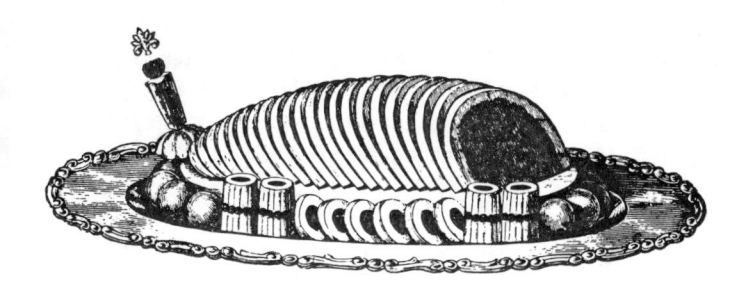

Manhattan: Midtown East
GIAMBELLI 50TH
Northern Italian

$$$

One of our smarter Italian restaurants in midtown, Giambelli 50th is always packed at luncheon and well filled at dinner. Lighting is romantically low, there are original paintings (apparently for sale) along the walls, and a staff that is friendly and efficient. The extensive menu gives house names to several specialties that are similar to classic dishes of the Italian cuisine. For example, *vitello silvano* is scaloppine with artichokes and peas, and *saltimbocca con carciofi e piselli* is the same veal with artichokes, peas and a thin strip of prosciutto. And both of these are not too different from *vitello Bolognese,* which is veal scaloppine with prosciutto and a strip of Fontina cheese. To my taste the best of the veal dishes is *vitello Principe Fillippo*— scaloppine with a strip of cheese and a tissue-thin layer of eggplant to give extra zip. Chicken, veal and beef dishes are almost all the same price, $12 à la carte. Soups are quite good, particularly minestrone, full bodied but not too starchy. Pastas, although expensive at $9, are beautifully done, especially a piquant spaghetti *Amatriciana*. Fried zucchini is among the best in New York, puffy, tender, non-greasy. Desserts are not exceptional, coffee is superb. The wine list is extensive, with moderately priced wines from nearly every region of Italy.

GIAMBELLI 50TH, 46 East 50th Street, Manhattan. Telephone: (212) 688-2760. Hours: 12-12, Monday-Friday; until 1 am, Saturday; closed Sunday. Cards: AE, BA/Visa, CB, DC, MC. Reservations required. Valet parking after 6. Full bar service.

Specialitá Casalinghe
Specialties of the House

LASAGNE VERDI PASTICCIATE
Baked Large Green Noodles 9.00

FETTUCCINE ALL'UOVO — Al Burro, Pomodoro,
Egg Noodles — o Bolognese
TAGLIERINI ALL'UOVO — Butter, Tomato
Thin Egg Noodles — or Meat Sauce
TAGLIATELLE VERDI
Green Egg Noodles 9.00

TRENETTE AL PESTO
Thin Egg Noodles with Pesto Sauce 9.00

LINGUINE "MARECHIARO" CON VONGOLE
Flat Spaghetti with Clam Sauce 9.00

SPAGHETTI "CACCIATORA" 9.00

SPAGHETTI "CARUSO" 9.00

SPAGHETTI "CARBONARA" 9.00

SPAGHETTI "AMATRICIANA" 9.00

DELIZIE DELLA "PASTORELLA" 9.00

PAGLIA E FIENO 9.00

RAVIOLI "PIEMONTESE"
Ravioli Old Piedmont Style 9.00

TORTELLINI AL SUGO DI CARNE
Chicken Dumplings, Meat Sauce 9.00

GNOCCHI "LOMBARDA"
Potato Dumplings with Sausage 9.00

CAPELLI D'ANGELO GRANZEOLA 14.00

CANNELLONI GRATINATI 9.00

CANNELLONI DI CARNE DI GRANCHIO
Crab Meat Cannelloni 9.00

MANICOTTI DI RICOTTA
Ricotta Cheese Manicotti with Tomato Sauce 9.00

COMBINATION (Cannelloni and Manicotti) 9.00

RISOTTO CON FUNGHI (All'ordine) 10.00

MOZZARELLA IN CARROZZA 9.00

CREPPELLE DI MELANZANE E RICOTTA 9.00

MELANZANE "PARMIGIANA"
Eggplant Parmigiana 9.00

Manhattan: Midtown East
GIAN MARINO
Italian
$$$

If you have dined even once at this restaurant, you were no doubt charmed by its omnipresent owner, the dapper Gian Marino or his younger, equally suave partner, Giovanni di Saverio. In particular, Gian Marino bobs from table to table, suggesting and asking for critical comment. He is proud of what he has: an excellent restaurant, with high standards of service, cuisine and ambience. Although Marino's roots are in Sicily, there are specials from the cuisines of Rome, Venice, Naples and Bologna on the expensive à la carte menu. Hot antipasto, generous enough for two, includes standard Italian favorites; a difference is in the seasoning, definitely present, but always suggestive rather than aggressive. Of the excellent soups, *pastina in brodo* is a personal favorite—its little pasta dots surprisingly al dente, despite their bath of heady, herby broth. One of my tests of any Italian kitchen is *pasta alla carbonara;* here it is costly ($5.75 at lunch, $8 at night), but worth the price. Other good pastas (which Gian likes to suggest) are those which feature tiny slivers of artichoke hearts, broccoli buds, or other seasonally fresh vegetables, in a delicate cream sauce. Veal and poultry are always of fine quality, and again sauces have character without being audacious. The Marino combination of veal and chicken with polenta, when on the menu, is always a treat. Queen of desserts is the platter of fresh fruits, selected at the market by Gian himself. Well-chosen Italian and French wines are available, at slightly higher prices than in most similar restaurants. Lunch is about $10 here; dinner at least $20.

GIAN MARINO, 221 East 58th Street, Manhattan. Telephone: (212) PL2-1696. Hours: 12-12, Monday-Friday; 4-12, Saturday; 1-11, Sunday. Cards: AE, BA/Visa, CB, DC, MC. Reservations suggested. Parking in nearby garage. Full bar service.

Piatti Del Giorno

Veal Scaloppine Mushrooms	8.50
Veal Parmigiana	8.25
Veal and Peppers	7.75
Veal Scaloppine alla Francese	8.50
Veal Cutlet Milanese con Osso	9.75
Calf's Brains au Gratin	7.50
Calf's Liver alla Veneziana	8.75
Sweetbreads Marsala	8.75
Veal Rollatine	9.00
Filet Mignon alla Pizzaiola	11.75
Filet Mignon Rollatine	12.00
Sliced Mignon Florentine	11.75
Sausages and Peppers alla Pizzaiola .	8.00
Trippa Con Risotto	7.25
Veal alla Casa	8.50
Stuffed Veal alla Valdostana with Mushrooms	11.75
Veal Piccata	8.50
Scaloppine Peppers Pizzaiola	8.50
Eggplant Parmigiana	6.75
Minute Steak Pizzaiola	11.75
Bocconcino di Manzo con Piselli ...	11.50

Manhattan: Midtown West
GIORDANO
Northern Italian

$$$

You need a nose keen as a truffle hound to find this hideout, tucked away on the fringe of Ninth Avenue at the mouth of the Lincoln Tunnel. By day this is a busy sector where you can shop in stall after stall with foodstuffs and spices from most sections of the globe spilling out onto the sidewalk. When the sun sets, the area is deserted. If you do find Giordano, however, there are happy surprises inside. Forty-eight tables are scattered among three rosy-red brick rooms and a sheltered garden patio. There are plenty of appetizers and some good soups. But pasta is the magnet that draws many diners. The noodles are mostly homemade and the sauces are concocted in a kitchen that really understands love Italian style. Several of the pasta dishes can be ordered in half portions, but why not order a full portion to share? That tart, tingly green, arugula, when in season is a lovely contrast to these rich sauces, but there are quite a few salads as well. For the main courses, all the great seafood, veal and chicken classics are available. (If you do not wish to wait half an hour for a dish to be prepared solely for you, check your choice with the waiter.) There are also desserts and cheeses, or you can end your meal with a cappuccino or a glass of mineral water. It's out of the tunnel and into a big meal at Giordano's, where lunch will average about $13 and dinner at least $20.

GIORDANO, 409 West 39th Street, Manhattan. Telephone: (212) 947-3883. Hours: 12-11, Monday-Friday; 5-12, Saturday; 2:30-10:30, Sunday. Cards: AE, BA/Visa, CB, DC, MC. Reservations suggested. Valet parking after 5:30 Monday-Saturday; after 2:30, Sunday. Full bar service.

VEAL CUTLET PARMIGIANA, MILANESE	8.25
VEAL SCALLOPPINE, MARSALA, PICATA	8.25
FRANCESE, BOLOGNESE, PIZZAIOLA	8.25
VEAL PALLIARD	8.25
BEEF PALLIARD (SIRLOIN)	10.50
CHICKEN IN WHITE WINE, MUSHROOM	8.25
PARMIGIANA, FRANCESE OR BROILED	8.25
CHICKEN SCARPARIELLO 30 MTE.	9.00
CHICKEN CACCIATORA 30 MTE.	9.00
BROILED SLICED FILET MIGNON	9.75
SLICED FILET AL MASALA, PIZZAIOLA	9.75
CHICKEN LIVERS SAUTE ONIONS & WINE	8.25
BOCCONCINI DI MANZO CON PISELLI	9.75
SALTINBOCCA ALLA ROMANA	8.50
BROILED FILET MIGNON	12.25
BROILED SIRLOIN STEAK	12.50
BROILED CALF'S LIVER, BACON OR VENEZIANA	8.25
SIRLOIN STEAK PIZZAIOLA	13.50
TRIPPA ALLA TRIESTINA	8.00
COSTATA DI VITELLO	10.25
CALAMARI IN BRODETTO	8.25
GAMBERI ALLA GRIGLIA, MARINARA, FRA DIAVOLO	9.75
LANGOSTINE MUGNAIA, MARINARA, FRA DIAVOLO	9.75
GAMBERI ALLA FIORENTINA, ARREGANATI	9.75
SCALLOPS BROILED OR SAUTE	8.50
BROILED FILET OR SOLE OR SAUTE, MUNIERE	8.25

Manhattan: Midtown East
GIRAFE
Northern Italian $$

They do not serve the long-necked animal here, although an intriguing metal cutout of the noble beast does stand guard out front. Nor do they serve lions, zebras or any of the other denizens of the veldt that watch you from giant wall photos. Despite this African kitsch, a leftover from previous occupants, there is a handsomeness about Girafe. Low-key lighting, decently spaced tables, professional and friendly service add up to an enjoyable dining experience. The kitchen here has evolved under different managements from a sort of Latin-Mediterranean-Italian to pure Italian. Pastas are taken quite seriously and the house is very proud of its *paglia e fieno* (straw and hay), the classic dish of green and white noodles intermingled with a light cream and cheese sauce. Not at all classic is Girafe's version of spaghetti carbonara. The *al dente* pasta comes laved generously in a tasty sauce with a chicken-broth base and no egg yolk—an interesting dish but not a true carbonara. Specials of the day are often good choices, such as veal Sorrentino, a delicate scaloppine with prosciutto, eggplant and mozzarella, topped with a light wine and tomato sauce. *Spigola a mare chiare* is representative of the quality of their fish dishes, which is high. This is delicate and fresh striped bass in a filmy batter, scented with lemon and wine. Desserts are made on the premises and are beautiful to see and to sample. Avoid the "jug" house wine and select from the small and decent wine list. À la carte lunch will average about $12; dinner about $18.

GIRAFE, 208 East 58th Street, Manhattan. Telephone: (212) PL2-3054. Hours: 12-3, 5:30-10:30, Monday-Thursday; 5:30-11, Friday-Saturday; closed Sunday. Cards: AE, BA/Visa, DC, MC. Reservations suggested. Parking in nearby garage. Full bar service.

Farinacei

Manicotti di Mozzarella	7.25	Canelloni Fiorentina	7.75
Lasagne al Forno	7.25	Vermicelli alle Vongole	8.00
Fettuccine Gioia	8.00	Spaghetti Carbonara	8.00
Trenette al Pesto	7.25	Fettuccine Alfredo	7.75
Paglia e Fieno	8.00	Fettuccine Verdi al Sugo	7.25
Spaghetti Bolognese	7.50	Fettuccine Filetto di Pomodoro	7.25
Tortellini alla Panna	7.50	Spaghetti Marinara	7.25
Gnocchi di Patate	7.50	Ravioli al Forno	7.50

Pesce

Spigola alla Livornese	9.00	Filetto di Sogliola Mugnaia	8.75
Zuppa di Pesce Veneziana	9.00	Scampi Saltati	9.00
Scampi Fra Diavolo	9.75	Scallops Amandine	8.75
Spigola al Brodetto	9.00	Calamari Luciana	8.00

Manhattan: Midtown East
GLOUCESTER HOUSE
Seafood
$$$

One of our more popular seafood palaces. If the steep prices do not deter you, it is possible to dine very well in this immaculate and airy establishment. For openers they repeatedly offer trays of oven-warm baking-powder biscuits. These high-rise breadstuffs are, save for a touch too much sugar, paragons of their kind. Special, too, is the Gloucester House Sauce for Oysters, a tart, slightly peppery accompaniment that appears on every table. The extensive menu is almost as bewildering to look at as a netful of seafood from the ocean floor. I find it better to ask the waiter to name a few of the daily specials. First, because if you go by the menu, your first choices are apt to be scratched that day, and also because the day's specials are certain to be the freshest of fish. A flaw here is that the service, while friendly, seems overly casual for prices that should provide smart professionalism. Everything is à la carte, with some fish dishes starting at about $9. There is a good wine list with whites that go well with all the catch.

GLOUCESTER HOUSE, 37 East 50th Street, Manhattan. Telephone: (212) PL5-7394. Hours: 12-2:30, 5:30-10, Monday-Friday; 12-10, Saturday-Sunday. Cards: AE, BA/Visa, CB, DC, MC. Reservations suggested. Street parking. Full bar service.

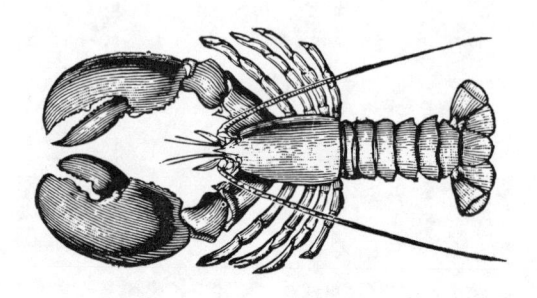

Crab Meat (*Au Gratin Style*)	15.50
Crab Meat (*Norfolk Style*)	15.50
Deviled Crabs	15.50
Crab Meat Newburg	16.25
Smithfield Ham, Crab Meat	16.25
Crab Meat Wrapped in Bacon	16.25
Lobster, Crab Meat au Gratin	18.25
Smoked Cod (*When Available*)	
(*Steamed*)	13.50
(*Broiled*)	13.50
(*English Style*)	14.25
(*Au Gratin*)	13.50
Finnan Haddie and Sea Scallops au Gratin	14.75
Shrimp Sauté	15.50
Fried Shrimp	15.50
Roast Shrimp, Garlic Butter	15.50
Shrimp Newburg	16.25
Shrimp Wrapped in Bacon	16.25
Sauté Guilfords (*When Available*)	12.50
Red Snapper Amandine	16.50

Manhattan: Midtown East
HERMITAGE
French Seafood $$

The flower-decorated walls simulate a country retreat, but those tiny "windows" are mirrors reflecting an elegant room with crisp linens, sparkling glassware, fresh flowers, and all sorts of precious antiques and gewgaws in little niches. Those mirrors, plus a low ceiling, make for annoying reverberations when the place is full, which is often the case. The little bar area is one of the most pleasing in town. One of the partners tends the bar; the other is an ever-present and alert host, suggesting treats and asking if everything is up to scratch. Aside from the sonic boom, everything usually is. The French food here is strong with the tang of the sea. From among the hors d'oeuvre, try the *bass froid, sauce gribiche,* made of mashed hard-cooked egg, mustard, herbs and vinegar. Among the soups, try the *soupe de poisson,* braced with *ailloli,* the garlic mayonnaise of Provence. A specialty is red snapper in a pungent broth, adorned by a few juicy mussels and accompanied by a sauce béarnaise. *L'entrecôte au vinaigre* is a handsome slab of fine beef, precisely as pink as you specify, with a lightly tart Bordelaise sauce. Vegetables, ethereally puréed, deserve an accolade. The wine list, while spare, has been assembled with discrimination, and lists a few bargains. Desserts are unusually good; coffee is excellent. À la carte entrées, at dinner, are priced from $11.75 to $17.50.

HERMITAGE, 251 East 53rd Street, Manhattan. Telephone: (212) 421-5360. Hours: 12-2:30, 6-10:30, Monday-Saturday; closed Sunday. Cards: AE, DC. Reservations required. Parking in nearby garage. Full bar service.

Hermitage

Dinez

Les Hors d'Oeuvres

Terrine de Poisson 4.25	Pâté de Campagne 4.75	Artichaut Vinaigrette 3.25
Anguille Fumé 3.75	Moules à la Russe 2.95	Melon & Jambon 4.60
Truite Fumée 4.25	Cocktail de Crevettes 4.75	Crabmeat Hermitage 8.50
Bluepoints 3.75	Saumon Romanoff 15.50	Little Necks 3.75
Hors d'Oeuvres Variés 5.50	Caviar de Beluga 22.00	Le Bass Froid, Sauce aux Herbes 4.50

Mousse de Brochet au Poivre Vert 5.25	Potage du Jour 2.75	Bisque de Homard 3.75
Barquette de Fruits de Mer 4.75	Soupe de Poisson 3.75	Cressonière Froide 3.00

La Spécialité du Jour

La Timbale de Homard Robert 17.50	L'Escalope de Saumon Hermitage 15.75
La Coquille St. Jacques au Poivre 11.50	Red Snapper, Sauce Beurnaise 14.00
La Sole Belle Meunière 14.50	Le Bass Rayé du Jour 11.75
Les Crevettes Espagnole Provençale 15.50	La Poularde à l'Estragon 11.75

L'Escalopine aux Cêpes 12.75
L'Entrecôte au Vinaigre 16.50
Le Turbot poché Hollandaise 16.50

Salade d'Endive, Cresson et Bibb 2.75

Tarte aux Fruits 3.00		Les Glaces et Sorbets 2.75
La Macédoine de Fruits 2.75		Mousse au Chocolat 3.00
Le Gateau du Jour 3.50	Coupe Hermitage 3.50	Le Gateau au Fromage 3.50

Le Brie et le St. André 3.25

Café Pompadour 3.25 Café Filtre 1.35 Sanka 1.00 Thé 1.00 Infusion 1.00

Manhattan: Midtown East
HUNAM
Chinese (Hunan)

$

Hunam is to other restaurants serving Hunan cooking what China is to Japan. China invented just about everything from ice cream to catsup, and Japan refined and elaborated on them. The Hunam restaurant proclaims it was the first in New York to serve this spicy, pungent cooking, yet somehow it does not seem so glorious today as in the beginning—perhaps because many other establishments have borrowed from the cuisine, although none serves food exactly like The Hunam. Despite an unevenness of quality, nothing ever seems to have been tamed down to suit the mythical American taste. An example of Hunam's authenticity is the Hunam preserved duck. When I chose it, the waiter indicated my colleague, an Oriental, and said: "That gentleman would like this dish, but have you ever had it before? It's fatty and quite salty." He was right. The dish was deliberately made that way, as it is in China. Yet the bony duck chunks with fatty skin, on a bed of bland chopped pork, is an interesting dish that mates well with vegetables or spicy foods. Eggplant family style is also made differently here; it comes in large shiny blocks and is quite piquant. Variations on classic themes are the superb Hunam pan-fried noodles with strips of chicken and other meats, water chestnuts and snow peas; and hot and sour fish broth. Seafood items of note are baby shrimp with pine nuts, shrimp puff in ginger sauce, and translucent fish filets, a non-spicy dish. If you order stuffed honey crisp banana, make sure it is the glacéed version and not a rather tasteless fritter. High-price specialty dishes range from $6.50 for shredded lamb tripe to $10.50 for whole sea bass.

HUNAM, 845 Second Avenue, Manhattan. Telephone: (212) 687-7471. Hours: 11:30-11, Sunday-Thursday; until 1 am, Friday-Saturday. Cards: AE, CB, DC. Reservations suggested. Parking in nearby lot. Full bar service.

Hunam Specialties

SLICED LEG OF LAMB, Hunam Style 7.25
Choice spring lamb with scallions and hot pepper sauce

GENERAL CHING'S CHICKEN 6.95
General Ching, the renowned General of the Chung Dynasty trained the famous Hunam Army. Chicken chunks with tingling Hot Sauce

LAKE TUNG TING SHRIMP 7.95
Giant Shrimp marinated with broccoli, ham, bamboo shoots and mushrooms in a white sauce (Lake Tung Ting is the largest lake in China)

HUNAM BEEF 7.75
Fillet of beef garnished with fresh water cress in a hot sauce

HUNAM'S HONEY HAM 8.75
China's finest preserved ham, honey glazed with lotus nuts

SPICY CRISPY WHOLE SEA BASS 10.50
Sea Bass, deep fried till crisp coated with Hunam hot sauce

BAMBOO STEAMER'S SPARERIBS 7.25
An authentic Hunam specialty. Baby spareribs marinated in hot sauce coated with rice flour. Steamed in a bamboo steamer

NEPTUNE'S PLATTER 9.75
An assortment of culinary sea treasures with crisp Chinese vegetables

HUNAM PRESERVED DUCK 7.75
Young preserved duckling steamed on a bed of marinated lean pork patties

FILLET OF SEA BASS with SHRIMP ROE SAUCE 7.75
Sea Bass fillet sauteed in a hot shrimp roe sauce

SHREDDED LAMB TRIPE 6.50
Authentic Hunam country style cooking. Shredded lamb tripe sauteed in hot Hunam Sauce

GENERAL GAU'S DUCKLING 7.75
Boned Duckling with button mushrooms and Chinese five spices in red hot sauce.

Manhattan: Midtown East
HUNGARIA
Hungarian
$$

Most Hungarian restaurants in New York are of the "mom and pop" variety and in the upper East Side. Hungaria, in the new Citicorp Center, is alive with the gusto of the *czardas* (country inns) of Hungary. At nights a live band—complete with tinkling cimbalon and crying violin—plays gypsy music intermingled with Viennese melodies and a bit of goodtime jazz. The menu is amusing and as complicated as a picture puzzle. There is an announcement of "free chewing bones, if we have them"; the bones are meatless, but lush with marrow to be scooped onto utterly delicious breads. The "Student Lunch: A Big Portion of Leftovers," offers such bounty as chewy oven-roasted veal shanks for only $3.75, the day after they have been a dinner feature at $10.50. Soups are as nourishing as good peasant potages should be. Stuffed cabbage appears in several forms; spaetzle, sausages and rosy paprika are prevalent. The more authentic and unusual the dish, the better it is likely to be—wild boar with sauerkraut, for example, or stuffed dilled cabbage with pork chops and sausage. The chefs all came from Hungary; a few do not speak English, but their "paprikash" is perfect. Desserts are incredible: an almost endless variety of *palacsintas* (crêpes) and pastries—crunchy puff pastes, nut-filled strudels, seven-layer cakes, and luscious creamy chocolate cakes, to name the barest few. The wine list is an adventure in itself, with Hungarian wines, both sweet and dry, at a modest $8. Hearty lunches are about $7.50; heartier dinners about $10 upwards. Don't sit too close to the music.

HUNGARIA, 153 East 53rd Street, Citicorp Center, Manhattan. Telephone: (212) 755-6088. Hours: 12-11:30, Monday-Thursday; until 2 am, Friday-Saturday; 1-9, Sunday. Cards: AE, BA/Visa, DC, MC. Reservations required. Street parking. Full bar service.

> Poached "Blue" Trout, Steamed New
> Potatoes, Brown Butter 9.75
> *Kékpisztráng fött burgonyával*

Fishermen's Broth with Paprika Carp,
Kettle Service 8.50
Halászlé bográcsban

TRADITIONAL DISHES

Oven Roasted Veal Shank, Szapary Style 10.50
Borjucsülök Szapáry módon

Medallion of Venison with Plum Sauce,
Pheasant Dumplings 12.50
Őzszeletek fácángombóccal

Stir-Fried Calf's Liver with Onion & Green
Pepper, Kalocsa Style 8.25
Gyors-pirított borjúmáj kalocsaiasan

Paprika Chicken with Egg Dumplings
a la Evike 7.25
Csirkepaprikás galuskával Évike módján

CABBAGE SPECIALTIES

Wild Boar Ragout with Dilled Sauerkraut 11.50
Vaddisznó paprikás káposztásan

Layered Cabbage Obuda Style 7.50
Rakott káposzta óbudai módon

Manhattan: Midtown East
IL CAMINETTO
Northern Italian
$$$

El Caminetto means the "little fireplace" and one burns cheerfully in a corner of this neat, warm restaurant when the season warrants. Such a name suggests coziness, and it is a tribute to Il Caminetto that a warm family feeling pervades the place yet in no way interferes with the most rigid standards of fine Italian cooking. Nino and his petite blonde wife, Roselle, have created what might be the very best Italian restaurant in Manhattan. Marcello, who greets you at the door with a smile of pleasure, is both maître d' and captain. His operatic gestures when he describes a dish are a great stimulant to the appetite. The waiters, quietly professional, still have time for a friendly smile or genial word. Most Italian restaurants, even fine ones in Italy, serve dishes with sauces that are all cousins, red or white. Here, every dish seems to have a sauce concocted exclusively for it, delicate, fragrant, precisely suitable. Nino's pasta dishes

PESCI

Casseruola di gamberi "all'americana"	8.00
Zuppa di pesce alla "Nino"	8.75
Scampi alla griglia con aglio	9.00
Cappe sante alla mugnaia o alla marinara	7.25
Spigola al "Golfo di Napoli"	8.00
Filetto di sogliola alla mugnaia	7.00

DALLA GRIGLIA

Paillard di vitello	9.25
Paillard di bue	11.00
Costata di bue	11.00
Costolette d'agnello	9.50
Trancia di fegato all'inglese	8.50
Filetto di bue	11.50

are superb, particularly one of his inventions, *I Golosi* (little gluttons). These are airy gnocchi, made from cream puff paste, bathed in a tantalizing sauce. Other pastas are also outstanding. The Stendahl Choice varies between chicken Sorrentina, skinless white meat, cooked in an ethereal white wine sauce and topped with a little prosciutto and a tissue of eggplant, and *costeletta di vitello "Sassi"* (at $9.25, the most expensive veal dish on the menu). This is a very thin, large chop of finest white veal, golden in an egg batter, garnished with a bit of black truffle, some fresh artichoke, and laved in a sauce of wine and brandy. Most other entrées are priced under $9. In addition to being chef, Nino is also a master pastry-maker. Try his *zuppa inglese* or one of his marvelous chocolate tortes and you will be convinced.

IL CAMINETTO, 202 East 50th Street, Manhattan. Telephone: (212) 758-1775. Hours: 12-3, 5:30-10:30, Monday-Friday; 5:30-11, Saturday; closed Sunday. Cards: AE, BA/Visa, CB, DC, MC. Reservations required. Street parking. Full bar service.

CARNI

Suprema di pollo "Sorrentina"	8.00
Intingolo di pollo "Scarpariello"	7.50
Intingolo di pollo "In tecia" con carciofi e prosciutto	7.75
Pollo alla Jacone	7.50
Saltimbocca alla romana	8.25
Scaloppine di vitello alla francese	7.75
Piccata di vitello al limone	7.75
Costoletta di vitello "Sassi"	9.25
Animelle dorate con funghi e capperi	8.50
Fegato di vitello alla veneziana	8.50
Fegatini di pollo al marsala e funghi	7.00
Medaglioni di filetto con funghi e peperoni	11.00
Filetto di bue "Rossini"	12.00

Manhattan: Midtown East
IPERBOLE/ROMA DI NOTTE
Italian
$$

Perhaps the handsome Roman, toga clad, who guards the door is a symbol of Janus, two-faced god of portals. Of portals there are two: At ground level is the restaurant Iperbole, Italian moderne, with metal sculptures, ornate chandeliers and, sometimes at night, strolling guitarists. Below ground lies Roma di Notte, the scene of a large dance floor, a live band, an open dining area and a maze of tiny caves reached by a winding footpath. The menu at Iperbole is larger than that of Roma di Notte, but if it isn't a busy night, you can select from the best of both. Appetizers, soups and pastas are the strong points, but do not expect classic versions of the latter. Each dish has a personal touch and all are quite carefully prepared. Most main dishes are all right but not extraordinary. The thing that makes Iperbole/Roma unique is a full menu page of a dozen quail specialties. These range from simple grilled quail on sliced French bread with a side of first-rate fried zucchini to a devilled quail served with diced eggplant and potato purée. Desserts, made on the premises, are not outstanding. Pastas range from $5.50 to $7.20, meat dishes from $8.50 to $11.50. Wines are priced at about $1 above most Italian restaurants, but there is a knowledgeable selection, including some fine wines of the Valtellina.

IPERBOLE, 137 East 55th Street, Manhattan. Telephone: (212) 759-9720. Hours: 12-12, Monday-Friday; 6-12, Saturday; closed Sunday. Cards: AE, CB, DC. Reservations suggested. Parking in nearby garage. Full bar service. ROMA DI NOTTE is open only for dinner and has its own telephone number: (212) 832-1128.

Rosette di Vitello "Sette Colli" **6.20**
(Veal Scaloppine "Seven Hills")

Piccata di Vitello al Limone. **5.95**
(Veal Piccata Sauteed with Lemons)

Scaloppine di Vitello alla Sorrentina. **6.20**
(Veal Scaloppine Sorrentina Style)

Saltimbocca alla Romana **6.10**
(Veal, Prosciutto, Sauteed in Wine)

Cotoletta alla Parmigiana **5.95**
(Veal Cutlet Parmigiana—Tomato Fleurs—Mozzarella)

Costoletta alla Milanese **5.80**
(Breaded Veal Cutlet)

Lombatina alla Sassi. **6.30**
(Milk Fed Veal Chop Sassi Style)

Lombata di Vitello ai Ferri **6.30**
(Milk Fed Veal Paillard)

Pollo alla Francese. **5.60**
(Chicken French Style)

Pollo All'Iperbole **5.80**
(Chicken Iperbole Style)

Intingolo di Pollo alla Romana. **5.60**
(Chicken Sauteed Roman Style Mushroom—Tomatoes—Pepper)

Pollo alla Arrabiata or Scarpariello **5.60**
(Chicken Saute—Garlic and Hot Peppers)

Omelette con Funghi o Fontina **4.95**
(Omelette Mushroom or Fontina Cheese)

Costolette Di Maiale Alla Griglia. **5.50**
(Loin of Pork Grilled)

Manzo Brasato al Barolo. **5.95**
(Beef Braised on Barolo Wine)

Fettine di Manzo "Pizzaiola". **8.50**
(Scaloppine of Beef "Pizzaiola")

Bistecca di Manzo ai Ferri. **9.50**
(Prime Broiled Sirloin Steak)

Cuore di Filetto di Bue. **9.50**
(Prime Filet Mignon)

Manhattan: Lower Midtown East
JACK'S NEST
Soul Food

$

This place has the bright-lit, bare-tabled look of a fast-food shop. And that is precisely what it is. What makes Jack's Nest unusual, however, is that it serves soul food, strictly soul food, and nothing but soul food. If you think soul food is chit'lins, barbecue, smoked ham hocks, collard greens, black-eyed peas and sweet potato pie, child, you are exactly right. That is what you get at Jack's Nest and plenty of them. A big plate of ribs with two vegetables, or a foil "basket" lined with French fries and topped with a fish dinner (fried flounder, shrimp and scallops), plus coffee or a soda will run about $6 apiece. I find the vittles very uneven in quality, but at these prices who's to quibble? All dinners come with hot corn bread and butter, and along with your paper napkin comes a "wet towel" packet. My suggestion is to skip the mashed candied yams (nearly tasteless) and stick with the collards—utterly delicious chopped greens, tart and piquant. My favorite main dish by far is the smothered chicken—juicy chicken pieces, very lightly crusted, then smothered in a flavorful brown onion gravy. Sweet potato pie does have flavor and appears with a thin, tasty crumb crust. Get seconds on the collards.

JACK'S NEST, 310 Third Avenue, Manhattan. Telephone: (212) 260-7110. Lunch: 11-3, Monday-Friday. Dinner: 3-11, Sunday-Thursday; until 2 a.m., Friday-Saturday. No credit cards. Reservations not accepted. Street parking. Full bar service.

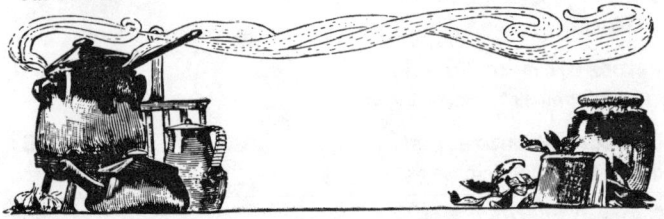

Manhattan: Midtown West
LA CARAVELLE
French $$$

This temple of gastronomy has long been one of the leading French restaurants in New York. Its standards have never flagged and menus are carefully planned so that there is a changing round of specialties. When last I dined there, the feature of the day, served from a silvery rolling cart, was roast veal as white as good bread, with leaf spinach cooked lightly enough to be Chinese. The dining area is warmly lighted with modest murals of Parisian scenes along the walls. Captains and waiters, while suavely professional, are also eminently human and likely to discourage you from ordering a dish that is not quite perfect. A must among the hors d'oeuvre is a Caravelle creation, *pain brochet de champenoise,* a thin pâté-like slice of fairy-delicate pike mousse, napped in a creamy champagne sauce, topped with mushroom caps and fried grapes. Characteristic of the light touch here, onion soup is quite delicate; its topping of finest Gruyère is melted but not browned. Meats and poultry are all of high quality. I especially like the duck with pepper, not the usual cliché *poivre verte,* but with a cream sauce, containing a few crushed black peppercorns; it is served with a lavish helping of wild rice. *Homard Washington* is unusual: lobster meat, perked with brandy and bourbon, served with a delicate cream-corn sauce. The wine book is a full one, with many excellent French choices. Before dessert your waiter offers a variety of interesting cheeses. Desserts are elegant and never too sweet. Lunches are *prix fixe* at $15.75, dinners are $26.75.

LA CARAVELLE, 33 West 55th Street, Manhattan. Telephone: (212) JU6-4252. Hours: 12:15-2:15, 6:15-10:15; Monday-Saturday; closed Sunday. No credit cards. Reservations required. Parking in nearby garage. Full bar service.

Manhattan: Midtown East
LA COTE BASQUE
French

$$$

This is not the magnificent restaurant of the days of Henri Soulé. These are different times, alas, when standards of dining out have been undermined by high prices, fast-food fetishes, and, in this case, loss of leadership. Soulé was never acclaimed for his lovability, but he was acclaimed, and rightly, for his stern generalship and severe ideals of what a temple of gastronomy must be. The place is still elegantly beautiful, with its warm murals, colorful tables and disciplined personnel. It is just that the rather simple menu (only nine choices on the *prix fixe* dinner) fails to impress, considering the prices demanded. Everything here is very good, but "very good" are words that should not be in the lexicon used to describe a restaurant where an evening meal is $28.50. A memory of the (literally) good old days lingers in the garlicky pâté that is the *terrine Côte Basque*. And some still maintain that the smoked salmon is the finest in the city. Every year *Forbes* magazine honors La Côte Basque with four stars, its highest rating. Sorry, I cannot concur.

LA CÔTE BASQUE, 5 East 55th Street, Manhattan. Telephone: (212) 688-6525. Hours: 12-3, 6-12; closed Sundays in July, Saturdays in August, and holidays. Cards: AE. Reservations required. Parking in nearby garage. Full bar service.

La Côte Basque

Dîner

Menu

Caviar Malossol 25.00　　　Saumon Fumé　　　Jambon de Bayonne
Melon　　Anguille Fumée　　Hors d'Oeuvre　　Cherrystones
Shrimps Cocktail　Melon Bayonne 1.75　Truite Fumée 1.50　Little Necks
Artichaut Vinaigrette　　Oysters in Season　　Grapefruit　　Jambon Persillé
Consommé　　Bisque de Homard　　Vichyssoise　　Saint Germain
Terrine Côte Basque　　Madrilène en Gelée　　Billy-By 1.75
Foie Gras Frais Prestige des Landes à la Gelée 12.00

Plats du Jour

QUARTIER D'AGNEAU RÔTI FAVORITE

POULARDE PÔELÉE BEAUSÉJOUR

MIGNONNETTES DE BOEUF SAUTÉES AUX ÉCHALOTTES

CANETON RÔTI AUX PECHES

CÔTE DE VEAU POJARSKY

RIS DE VEAU PRINCESSE

STRIPED BASS DUGLÉRÉ

SUPRÊMES DE SOLE DIPLOMATE

SOLE IMPORTÉE MEUNIÈRE DORIA

Spécialités (7.00 supp.) LES NOISETTES D'AGNEAU ÉDOUARD VII

LE COEUR DE FILET PÉRIGOURDINE　　　LA CÔTE DE VEAU AUX CÈPES
LES QUENELLES DE BROCHET ÉMINENCE　　LA SOLE SOUFFLÉE WALEWSKA
LES CÔTELETTES DE PIGEONNEAU SÉVIGNÉ
LE STEAK AU POIVRE　　LE TURBOT FRAIS POCHÉ BEURRE DE TRUFFE
LE POULET REINE SAUTÉ PETIT DUC　　LE HOMARD AU PORTO

Les Desserts Côte Basque
Ou Les Fromages

Spécialités Les Soufflés Tous Arômes 4.50 p.p.　Les Crêpes Côte Basque 4.00

Café 1.00　　　Demi Tasse 1.00　　　Filtre 1.00　　　Prix du Dîner 28.50

Manhattan: Upper East Side
LA FOLIE
French

$$$

The ingenious and mischievous designer George Lang has transformed a niche in the conservative Carlton House into La Folie —madness. The bar serves caviar by the pinch (Beluga, $12), along with a choice of Russian and Polish vodka, while you loll upon your tall lucite stool, taking care not to tread on the dozens of sculptured feet that protrude from under the bar. (In the men's room you can make a phone call seated on a giant silver hand.) To reach the elegant, candlelit dining room with its marble and mirrored walls, you step across a giant roulette table inlaid in marble. (This becomes the dance floor when La Folie turns into a disco in the late hours.) Madcappery abounds, but so does excellent food. Among the hors d'ouevre are smoked Scotch salmon and a terrine of duck tingling with Armagnac. *Le feuillete aux champignons* is a delightful mélange of mushrooms and herbs on a bed of feather-light puff pastry. All entrées sampled have been totally satisfying. I was astonished to see *le confit de canard* listed as a main dish; however, it was not just a fat-drenched tidbit, but slow-cooked pieces of duck served with excellent garlic-scented home fries. Vegetables are prepared with the crunch left in. If your childhood dream of sweets was a Mallowbar elevated to angelic heights, try the *negrillon spécialité de La Folie*. Coffee is splendid and so is the moderately priced wine list. There is a three-course lunch for $12.50; à la carte dinners average $25.

LA FOLIE, 21 East 61st Street, Manhattan. Telephone: (212) 765-1400. Hours: 12-3, 6-11, Monday-Friday; until midnight, Saturday; closed Sunday. Cards: AE, DC. Reservations suggested. Parking in nearby garage. Full bar service.

Hors d'Oeuvre

Smoked Scotch Salmon   7.50

La Terrine de Canard à l'Armagnac   5.00

Le Caviar Beluga Imperial d'Iran   18.00

Blue Point Oysters   5.00

Artichoke Stuffed with Seafood Remoulade   6.00

Little Neck Clams   4.50

Le Gratin de Homard   7.00

Hot Oysters au Champagne et Caviar   6.50

Les Moules du Maine à la Riche   4.00

Snail Pot Pie Bourguignonne   5.00

Entrées

Broiled Fresh Dover Sole au Beurre Blanc   16.00

Filet of Striped Bass with Fennel   15.00

Les Quenelles de Brochet Nantua   14.50

La Mousse de Sole Homardine   15.00

Le Confit de Canard   15.00

Les Ris de Veau Perigueux, en Croûte   15.00

Duckling Roasted with Three Fruits   15.50

Grenadins of Veal, Madison   16.00

Coeur de Filet aux Poivres Verts et Noirs   16.50

Médaillons of Beef Dijonnaise   15.00

Broiled Filet Mignon Deux Sauces   16.00

Rack of Lamb aux Herbes de Provençe (For Two)   29.00

Manhattan: Midtown East
LA GRENOUILLE
French $$$

Paul Masson was a delightful gentleman who made real his fantasy of a flower garden where one may dine. Wherever there are not heaps of exquisite flowers, there are mirrors to multiply their images. During M. Masson's lifetime, La Grenouille was a match in food and service for the illustrious Le Pavillon. Some of the sun left the flowers when he departed, although his family now does its best to maintain impeccable standards. Over the years tables have become a bit too squashed together for a place of such elegance, but La Grenouille still attracts customers who demand the best without caring about cost. Potages are delicate and deft. The assorted hors d'oeuvre are a mélange of fresh and interesting vegetables, and when shrimp remoulade is included, even New Orleanians admit it is better than down home. *Les grenouilles Provencale,* the frog legs that are the namesake of the establishment, are among the sweetest, freshest, plumpest you will ever taste. Vegetables come to the table as fresh as the flowers. Excellent as the main dishes are, the Stendahl Choice is a dessert (even though it costs extra). As soon as you are seated, request one of the *soufflés tous parfums.* They are all superb, but my favorite is the chocolate, an ethereal triple-taste treat: lightly crusty on top, foamy just below the surface, a gentle custard in the center. No other restaurant can match it. There are no bargains among the wines, but the selection is as radiant as the hand-selected bouquets above your table. Without wines, luncheons are *prix fixe,* $15.25; dinners $28.75.

LA GRENOUILLE, 3 East 52nd Street, Manhattan. Telephone: (212) PL2-1495. Hours: 12:15-2:45, 6:15-10:45, Monday-Saturday; closed Sunday. Cards: AE. Reservations suggested. Street parking. Full bar service.

State Street, 1864.

Manhattan: Upper East Side
LA PETITE FERME
French $$

When it was a tiny hole-in-the-wall in Greenwich Village, La Petite Ferme could be identified by the line standing outside waiting for a table. Now that it has moved to an elegant uptown location, there is a little more room (about 14 tables), but reservations are imperative. While there is no connection between La Petite Ferme and Chez Pascal, both are run by members of the family Chevillot, which has long operated a celebrated stop along the Burgundy trail, the Hôtel de la Poste of Beaune. "The little farm" achieves a fresh-scrubbed look with bare wooden tables, plaid napkins as big as dish towels, fresh flowers, a few wall cupboards, and a pair of cooing doves in a rustic cote. The menu (displayed on slates by a young and friendly staff) is limited to two meat and two fish dishes each day, with a few appetizers and desserts. *Potage Ardennaise* is unusual, a delicately creamed soup of endive. (It is served, as is everything hot here, on blistering plates of a beautiful blue on white rustic pattern.) *Moules vinaigrette* are also a typical beginning treat at La Ferme. Main dishes are beautiful rather than bountiful, leaving room on the plates for an artistic arrangement of crisply cooked fresh vegetables. I especially recommend the fish, which is cooked in a sensitive manner. I did not at all like a sticky chocolate mousse. The Chevillot family has its own vineyards back home and the popular wines here are from those vines, particularly the low-cost pleasant house white and red.

LA PETITE FERME, 973 Lexington Avenue, Manhattan. Telephone: (212) 249-3272. Hours: 12-2:30, 6-10:15, Monday-Saturday; closed Sunday. Cards: AE, BA/Visa, DC. Reservations suggested. Parking in nearby garage. Full bar service.

Manhattan: Midtown West
LARRE'S
French $

The prices at Larre's have made this remarkable family-run restaurant a mainstay for two generations of New Yorkers who enjoy good food but possess meager pocketbooks. Last time I counted there were at least 16 complete dinners below $10. The range of the menu is wide, and there may be almost a dozen worthwhile complete dinners around a modest $8 or so. The cooking is honest family-French. The place is simply decorated, light and airy, and while Larre's is almost always busy, it is also always professional. At the closely packed tables you will see young lovers, distinguished elderly persons, musicians and artists—now and again one you may recognize. Lorre's has almost no competition for doing what it does so well. Let us hope this landmark will remain with us forever. Lunches that include dessert and coffee range from $3.50 to $6. Dinners begin at a modest $6.50 and go up to $10.50 for a few of the more expensive items. All dinners include appetizer, salad and dessert.

LARRE'S FRENCH RESTAURANT, 50 West 56th Street, Manhattan. Telephone: (212) 974-9170 and 664-9414. Hours: 11:30-2:30, 5-9:30, Monday-Saturday; closed Sunday. Cards: AE, DC. Reservations accepted for six or more. Street parking. Full bar service.

Manhattan: Midtown East
LAURENT
French
$$$

Laurent is like a secret club. It is rarely publicized, yet I have never been here without finding almost every table filled. You enter through a characterless hotel corridor, descend a few steps and find a spacious, dark-wood bar area, a marvelously clubby place. Going into the dining room, you pass a great display of more hors d'oeuvre and desserts than is allowed on even Gargantua's diet. The ambience here reminds me of a dining room aboard a great ocean liner in the days when the elite travelled by sea. This restaurant, no larger than many, has a staff of 100, all determined to turn a meal into an occasion. Its slogan is: "When it's first in season, it's first at Laurent." The menu is both lavish and expensive, but I have never received less than I paid for, nor have I had a vegetable or meat served out of prime season. There are many dishes I might label Stendahl Choice, but I think my vote goes to the *petite marmite* (only $3.50) which is done in the classic tradition set forth by Escoffier, and duplicated almost nowhere else in this fast-food city. You are not merely served a fine vegetable-beef soup—your waiter extracts the meat and thin slices it on a carving board before he ladles the luscious broth. The wine list is exemplary. If you have doubts, seek the advice of the sommeliers, who are both knowledgeable (in New York not always to be taken for granted) and ready to share expertise without snobbery.

LAURENT, 111 East 56th Street, Manhattan. Telephone: (212) PL3-2729. Hours: 12-3:30, 6-10:30, Monday-Saturday; 5-10:30, Sunday. Cards: AE, DC. Reservations required. Parking in nearby garage. Full bar service.

Specialities de la Maison

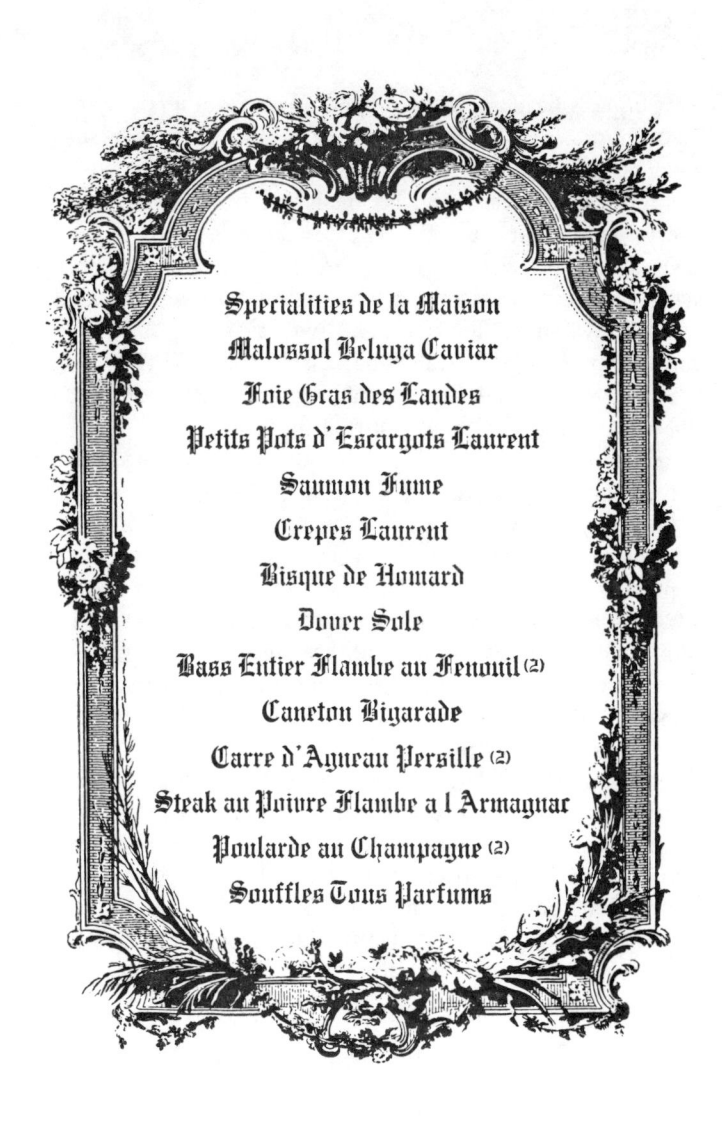

Malossol Beluga Caviar

Foie Gras des Landes

Petits Pots d'Escargots Laurent

Saumon Fume

Crepes Laurent

Bisque de Homard

Dover Sole

Bass Entier Flambe au Fenouil (2)

Caneton Bigarade

Carre d'Agneau Persille (2)

Steak au Poivre Flambe a l Armagnac

Poularde au Champagne (2)

Souffles Tous Parfums

Manhattan: Upper East Side
LE CIRQUE
French
$$$

Le Cirque is headquarters for the ultra-chic, yet no one can claim a special table, and everyone receives special treatment. Owners and staff alike have a zest for making each customer feel at ease, and do their best to anticipate his every need. The menu is chiefly classic French but there are always daily specials that surprise and generally delight. Pasta primavera was created here, and is now widely imitated elsewhere. Pasta is dressed with a creamy, buttery sauce with cheeses at tableside, then a mélange of fresh seasonal vegetables—broccoli buds, snow peas, quartered cherry tomatoes—is quickly stirred in. The crunch of the barely-done greens makes a heavenly marriage with the velvety pasta. Perfection. Another Stendahl Choice is *escalopes de veau sautées vielle France:* delicate scallops of whitest veal in a luscious cream sauce tipped with cognac, topped with a sculptured mushroom, served with a portion of excellent noodles. Presentation of every dish has an almost Japanese beauty. In all dishes only the best ingredients are used and the cooking is done with great care. The wine list is an elegant hand-lettered compilation of excellent choices at surprisingly reasonable prices. There is a treasure in the form of some ancient Burgundies that mysteriously sell for less than you would pay for them in a store, assuming you could even locate these gems from the thirties and fifties. Because of its fine foods, beautiful wines, and genuinely warm and subtle service, Le Cirque has always been a personal favorite. Luncheons are *prix fixe* at $11.50. Dinner averages about $25, plus wines. There is an annoying $1 cover charge at dinner.

LE CIRQUE, 58 East 65th Street, Manhattan. Telephone: (212) 794-9292. Hours: 12-3, 6-10:30, Monday-Saturday; closed Sunday. Cards: AE, DC. Reservations necessary. Street parking. Full bar service.

Specialites de la Maison

Carpaccio Toscana	5.75
Les Crepes Le Cirque	6.75
La Sole Anglaise Marguery	11.75
Le Cote de Veau Milanaise	12.95
Le Supreme de Volaille Gismonda	7.95
Entrecote (2) au Poivre Vert au Vinaigre de Bourgogne	29.50

Specialites de la Semaine

Lundi —	Le Canard Roti du Jour	9.75
Mardi —	Le Carre d'Agneau Roti aux Flageolets	12.95
Mercredi —	Le Poulet en Cocotte Grand Mere	8.75
Jeudi —	Fricandeau de Veau Roti, Chasseur	12.50
Vendredi —	Le Bar Raye Majestic	9.75
Samedi —	Le Contrefilet Roti avec Mousseline de Legumes	13.75

Special from the Charcoal Broiler

Cote de Veau Aplatie	12.95
Entrecote Minute Aplatie	13.25
Poulet Grille Diable	8.25
Selle de Pre Sale Desossee	12.75
Brochette de Rognon de Veau aux Herbes	9.50

Manhattan: Upper East Side
LE LAVANDOU
French $$

Le Lavandou is a small room, made to appear bigger by a mirror wall at one end. The tables are too close together, however, and the noise level when the room is full can be high. Aside from these flaws, the restaurant is just about perfect in all departments. The lighting from chandeliers and wall sconces is low enough to be flattering, but bright enough to illuminate your food. The staff is considerate and professional, and Luke, the young maître 'd/captain is as watchful as a bird. Finally, the food: Not even at temples of gastronomy charging twice these prices do you see such skillful presentation or taste such divine sauces. Chef Jean-Jacques Rachou is a true artist. From his immaculate kitchen comes a parade of dishes prepared with imagination, served with flair, and so beautiful that they belong in an art gallery. A trout is reconstructed with a puff-pastry crescent for a tail, and a mingling of leeks and asparagus tips to create head and eyes. White, butter-tender medallions of veal are a fantasy of garnishes—two dollops of spinach, a cheese-striped bit of broccoli, rosettes of puréed carrots and a cylinder of that seldom-served vegetable, salsify; a heavenly sauce, wrinkly with morels, comes on the side. Tender fish is bathed in a creamy champagne or sorrel sauce, in which a signature-like pattern is drawn by a thread of red wine. A dozen such creations may be ordered on the *prix fixe* dinner at $19.50. Included is a selection of 10 hors d'oeuvre, such as sole *en croûte* or quenelles with pernod, a lush dessert and *cafe filtre.* The three-course lunch is $10.50. There is a thoughtfully chosen wine list.

LE LAVANDOU, 134 East 61st Street, Manhattan. Telephone: (212) 838-7987. Hours: 12-2:30, 6-10, daily. Cards: AE. Reservations suggested. Parking in nearby garage. Full bar service.

Les Pâtés et Terrines à la gelée de Porto
Artichaut en Feuilles
Coupe de Fruits Rafraîchis
Le Saint Germain Paysanne
Le Grapefruit Suprême
Le Bisque de Homard

Les Fillets de Sole "Trois Gros"
Les Scallops aux Amandines
Le Saumon Glacé au Poivre Vert
Le Striped Bass à l'Oseille
La Croustade de Sea-Food Cardinale
La Sole Anglaise Belle Meuniére
La Breast of Capon en Jambonnette
Les Noisettes de Veau aux Morilles
Le Veal Kidney à la Bordelaise
Les Sweetbreads Braisé Varoise
La Suprême Façon Gismorda
Le Cassoulet du Chef Toulousain

Manhattan: Midtown East
LE MADRIGAL
French $$$

This favorite standby of the publishing and television worlds has undergone a change of chefs recently, but the good food has not been much altered, and the house specials have not changed. Le Madrigal features a long narrow room of banquettes beneath pastel murals of the Directoire era, and at the end, a small, snugly glassed mock greenhouse. Delightful in spring, when burgeoning limbs outside dance with new leaves. Although a few dishes are prepared with so light a hand that they approach blandness, this is not true of a *saucisse en croûte*, served as an appetizer—a long pastry roll encases a smartly spiced garlicky sausage, sliced in thin rounds and napped with a well-seasoned truffle sauce. When they are in season, try the elegantly slim asparagus with a deft, creamy vinaigrette. Potage unfortunately does not seem to attain the standards set by the hors d'oeuvre. Two house specials are the sautéed veal medallions with morels in champagne sauce and a tender beef filet spread with goose liver pâté, wrapped in a crêpe and served with a light green peppercorn sauce. Dinners, *table d'hôte*, range from $18.50 to $23. The luncheon menu is à la carte, and offers fewer choices. I have always enjoyed the sole with tangy fresh tartar sauce. The almost totally French wine list offers an excellent Sancerre at $11.75 and a Château Simard, '71, at $13.

LE MADRIGAL, 216 East 53rd Street, Manhattan. Telephone: (212) 355-0322. Hours: 12-3, 6-10:30, Monday-Saturday; closed Sunday. Cards: AE, DC. Reservations suggested. Parking in nearby garage. Full bar service.

HORS D'OEUVRES

Jambon de pays et melon 2.00
Saucisson chaud
Feuilleté jambon et fromage
Bouquet de crevettes 2.25
Little necks
Blue points
Crab meat Madrigal 6.00
Saumon fumé de Gaspé 2.25
Truite fumée 1.50
Les trois terrines
Crêpes de fruits de mer 3.00
Foie-gras des Landes 9.50
Caviar de la Caspienne sur glace 20.00

ENTRÉES

Escalope de veau à l'orange 20.00
Escalope de veau aux girolles 22.00
Ris de veau aux girolles 20.00
Pojarsky au vieux Bordeaux 18.50
Mignon de veau aux morilles 23.00
Rognons de veau au champagne 19.00
Carré d'agneau aux primeurs 23.00
Poularde châtelaine 18.50
Poularde aux morilles 22.50
Canard aux pommes et poivre vert 19.00
Caneton à l'orange 19.00
Pigeonneau en cocotte 22.00
Coeur de filet en chemise au poivre vert 22.50
Steak au poivre Clermont 22.50
Tournedos forestière 23.00

Manhattan: Midtown East
LE MARMITON
French $

Le Marmiton is an agreeable exception to the prevailing feeling that Manhattan's French restaurants have lost their *joie de vivre*. The place is always filled, at lunchtime with a large contingent from the publishing world, and nights with many who seem as regular as boarders. Service is not only friendly but attentive. I do, however, have a slap on the wrist for Le Marmiton—women dining alone or casually dressed are often shunted to a dining room in the rear. Low rustic beams, Limoges plates and lacquer-shiny copper pots build the feeling of a French country inn. There is a specialty that never appears on the menu, but is often on hand to please homesick Francophiles: a down-home blood sausage, thoroughly good. In warm weather the Stendahl Choice is duckling *à l'orange en gelée,* chilled duck meat imbedded in glossy gelatin with a slice of orange in the center. Pretty as a flower and delicious. In general, the heartier the dish the better the food. *Saucisson maison* is a hot, spicy sausage with lightly oiled rounds of potatoes that would make a *grandmère* proud. Hearty, too, is the *boeuf sauté Bourguignon,* the winey sauce crying out to be sopped with bread crusts. The house special dessert is a luscious creamy mousse with almonds. There are two special miniature menus at Le Marmiton. From 5 to 7 there is a special complete meal for a very low $8.75, perfect for pre-theater dining. On Saturday night there is a Champagne Dinner, a full meal with a choice of entrées, plus a bottle of excellent French champagne, all for only $35 per couple.

LE MARMITON, 216 East 49th Street, Manhattan. Telephone: (212) MU8-1232, MU8-1355. Hours: 12-3, 5-10, Sunday-Friday; until 11, Saturday. Cards: AE, BA/Visa, CB, DC, MC. Reservations suggested. Parking garage nearby. Full bar service.

Jefferson Market Courthouse, Sixth Avenue, 1885.

Manhattan: Midtown East
LE PERIGORD
French $$

While midtown east is the site of many French restaurants, it is rare to find one way over beyond First Avenue. But Le Perigord offers superior French cuisine in this unbusy residential area. This is the father of Le Perigord Park and I prefer quiet old dad to the more polished son—possibly because Le Perigord is homey, like a French hotel restaurant, rather than like a Park Avenue French restaurant. The dining room is an open square without much adornment or charm. On busy weekends, when customers overflow into the back room, I like to dine in this cozy rear area, with its French countryside murals and its own little bar. On quiet weeknights, however, you may find your group the only diners here. In both dining areas, service is courteous but occasionally the tiniest bit forgetful; don't be surprised if you have to pour your own wine. The wine list, incidentally, has some nice choices: Château de Sancerre '74 at only $10, Château L'Angelus '71 at $14 and a good Alsatian

---

Bouillabaisse du Vieux Port 20.00

Truite Grenobloise 16.00

Grenouilles Provençale 19.00

Gratin de Langoustines 19.50

Homard Monte-Carlo 22.00

Sole Ambassadeur ou Grillé 18.50

Turbot Poché Sauce Mousseline 21.00

Entrecôte au Poivre Vert ou Marchand de Vin 20.50

Tournedos Rossini 23.00

Chateaubriand Béarnaise (pour 2) 39.00

Riesling at $9. The menu is classic French. An hors d'oeuvre of striped bass remoulade is flaky tender with an airy homemade mayonnaise. And *potage ambassadeur* is definitely a diplomat among pea soups. Entrées that come on heaping plates include *medaillon de veau Archduc,* a thin cutlet of excellent veal, touched with wine-cream gravy with mushrooms; and *ris de veau braisé aux petit pois,* braised sweetbreads with baby peas. On a recent night, roast beef *perigourdine* was the special; the beef was good, rare as ordered, but I longed to spy a few more black truffle dots in the sauce. Desserts include a fine chocolate mousse, freshly made fruit tarts and dusky, lovely crème caramel. Luncheons are about $12 and *table d'hôte* dinners range from $16 to $21.50.

LE PERIGORD, 405 East 52nd Street, Manhattan. Telephone: (212) PL5-6244. Hours: 12-3, 6-10:30, Monday-Friday; 6-10:30, Saturday; closed Sunday. Cards: AE, DC. Reservations recommended. Parking in nearby garage. Full bar service.

Poulet rôti à l'Estragon 16.00

Poularde Poëlée au Champagne 16.50

Canard aux Pêches, Riz Sauvage 18.00

Pigeon en Cocotte aux Olives 19.50

Médaillon de Veau Archiduc 18.50

Rognon de Veau à la Moutarde 16.00

Côte de Veau Poëlée aux Cèpes 21.50

Ris de Veau Braisé aux Petits Pois 16.00

Côtes d'Agneau Grillées 18.50

Carré d'Agneau Rôti Persillé (pour 2) 37.00

Manhattan: Upper East Side
LE PERIGORD PARK
French $$

The offspring of Le Perigord is more opulent, more formal and a bit more expensive than the original. Both restaurants have the same owners, however; both kitchens are supervised by the same master executive chef; and in general the food at both is much the same. There are three levels at Le Perigord Park: a main dining room, light and airy, suggesting the French Riviera in decor; a more intimate section near the bar; and a smaller rear section to catch the overflow. Service is not haughty, but is definitely more reserved and superior to that of the smaller parent restaurant. The menu is more elaborate also, and while luncheons at both places are in the same price range, *table d'hôte* dinners at the Park hover around the $20 mark. Truffles, the pride of Perigord, appear here in a house specialty, *canard laque aux endives et truffes noires,* duckling with endive and black truffles. Roast veal is often a special *plat du jour* and is generally moist and good. *Homard dans sa carapace au whiskey* is an unusual whiskey-sauced lobster meat in the shell. And *entrecôte au poivre vert à l'Armagnac et crème* is one of the richer versions of this heady green-pepper steak. Desserts are sisters of the original restaurant.

LE PERIGORD PARK, 575 Park Avenue, Manhattan. Telephone: (212) PL2-0050. Hours: 12-3, 6-11, Monday-Friday; 6-11, Saturday-Sunday. Cards: AE, DC. Reservations suggested. Parking in nearby garage. Full bar service.

Entrées

NAVARIN DE RED SNAPPER ET HOMARD AUX PETITS LÉGUMES 21.00

LA NAGE DE COQUILLE ST. JACQUES 19.00

SOLE ANGLAISE AU SABAYON D'OSEILLE 19.00

BASS POCHÉ AUX AROMATES ET BEURRE ROUGE 18.50

BEURRECK DE CRAB-MEAT 20.00

FOIE GRAS DE CANARD SAUTÉ AUX ÉCHALOTTES ET VINAIGRE DE FRAMBOISES 21.00

CANARD LAQUÉ AUX ENDIVES ET TRUFFES NOIRES 20.00

POULARDE POÊLÉE AU PORTO-COULIS DE CÈPES — POMME DOUCE 19.50

PIGEON GRILLÉ — DIABLÉ À NOTRE FAÇON 20.00

CÔTE DE VEAU À LA CRÈME AIGRE — BARQUETTES DÉLICE — PRUNEAUX 20.00

POULET SAUTÉ SAUCE ROUILLEUSE 18.50

Manhattan: Upper East Side
LES PLEIADES
French $$

The little bar is papered with handsome posters from art dealers; the famous Parke-Bernet and other galleries are nearby. If you are gallery hopping, Les Pleiades makes a nice luncheon stop. It is pleasant for dinner, too, with its red walls, large paintings of French scenes, romantic lighting and well-spaced tables. Both luncheon and dinner menus are interestingly grouped into price categories; luncheon choices are $6.50 and $7.50 and the dinner entrées are $9.25, $10.50 and $13.50. There are also about 15 hors d'oeuvre, priced at $2.50 midday, and at $3 in the evening. When asparagus is in season, it commands the list; the juicy fat spears are served either hot with a delicate hollandaise or cold with a very light vinaigrette. The *pâté maison* seems too fatty to my taste; a garlicky sausage in crust is better. Among the luncheon dishes offered is *la cervelle au beurre noir,* brains sautéed with brown butter and capers. A standout at lunch or dinner is *le navarin d'agneau printanière,* a lamb stew packed with carrots, peas and other fresh vegetables in a luscious dark sauce. *Le bass a l'oseille* is tender and napped with a suave sorrel sauce; and *le foie de veau meunière,* calf's liver, was declared by one afficionado as being the best ever tasted. Desserts are homemade. A fruit tart is nice and the Napoleon slice contains good light pastry cream, but the *mille-feuille* is sometimes a bit tough. The owner of Les Pleiades is Basque and he offers the Basque Izarra, a piquant Chartreuse-like liqueur. There is also a moderately priced wine list.

LES PLEIADES, 20 East 76th Street, Manhattan. Telephone: (212) 535-7230. Hours: 12-3, 5:30-11, Monday-Saturday; closed Sunday. Cards: AE, BA/Visa, MC. Reservations suggested. Parking in nearby garage. Full bar service.

your choice $9.25

LE PLAT DU JOUR

LA TIMBALE "PLEIADES"
 mixed sea food, white wine

LE BASS A L'OSEILLE
 poached bass, sorrel sauce

LE NAVARIN D'AGNEAU PRINTANIERE
 lamb stew, mixed vegetables

LE POULET ROTI A L'ESTRAGON
 roast chicken, tarragon sauce

ROGNONS DE VEAU GRILLES DIJONNAISES
 broiled veal kidneys, mustard sauce

your choice $10.50

LA SOLE ANGLAISE GRILLEE, SAUCE MOUTARDE
 broiled dover sole, mustard sauce

LES GRENOUILLES PROVENCALES
 frogs' legs "saute" with garlic

LE FOIE DE VEAU MEUNIERE
 calf's liver "saute" meuniere

LES CREVETTES A LA NICOISE
 scampi saute, garlic & tomatoes

Manhattan: Midtown East
LE VEAU D'OR
French
$$

Multitudes love Le Veau d'Or; a few shun it. It has an over-busy Left Bank bistro ambience, with tables so close together you might almost eat off someone else's plate. Waiters imperturbably skitter along non-existent aisles, never spilling more than a drop. It's always jammed and at peak hours reservations are honored a little less than promptly. Obviously, this kind of crowd feeding turns some diners off; obviously, it turns more diners on. The golden calf has been more like a golden goose for many long years. For those who do not mind mixing din with their dining, the reward is good honest French cooking at prices below those of quieter, more pretentious Gallic establishments. The menu is not lengthy, but cooking time for its items quite often is. *Tripes à la mode de Caen* is a cliché on most French menus; here the dish is lovingly slow cooked to get maximum flavor from its ingredients. There is a similar serious application to traditional country cooking in such things as *poussin rôti en cocotte "grand' mère,"* a little brown-roasted chicken in a good sauce; and, when it is available, *civet de lapin,* in which the dark sauce on the rabbit is properly thickened with blood, not flour. Luncheons average about $9; complete dinners range from $11.50 to $14.

LE VEAU D'OR, 129 East 60th Street, Manhattan. Telephone: (212) 838-8133. Hours: 12-2:30, 6-10:15, Monday-Saturday; closed Sunday. No credit cards. Reservations suggested. Street parking. Full bar service.

Filets de Hareng, à la Crème
Céleri Remoulade • Canapé Maison
Sardines Importées • Maquereau au Vin Blanc
Pâté du Chef

Potage Cressonnière • Consommé aux Pâtes
Soupe à l'Oignon Gratinée

Filet de Sole Sauté Amandines	11.50
Grenouilles Sautées Provençale	13.50
Homard Grillé au Beurre Fondu, (entier)	
Gigot d'Agneau Rôti Bretonne	12.10
Canard Rôti aux Cerises, Riz Sauvage	13.50
Poussin Rôti en Cocotte, "Grand'Mère"	12.10
Foies de Vollaille Poëlés Lyonnaise	12.10
Tripes à la Mode de Caen	12.10
Rognon de Veau Sauté Moutarde	13.10
Sauté de Veau Niçoise	12.10
Filet de Boeuf Rôti, Sauce Champignons	14.90
La Douzaine d'Escargots Bourguignonne	13.90
Carré d'Agneau Soissonnais (2)	33.00

Manhattan: Midtown East
L'OLIVIER
French

$$$

There is an oddity about L'Olivier. Appetizers and soups seem to lack that tantalizing extra something that makes a dish memorable, but I have found most of the main dishes outstanding. As always, however, there is an exception to the generality—one appetizer, *feuillette de Roquefort*, is an elegant puff pastry that gushes forth a creamy froth of cheese when pierced. Beautiful! Of the entrées, sweetbreads with morels make a heavenly combination. Huge and hearty but worth their calories are *cassoulet maison*, white beans, goose, meats and sausage in wine sauce, and *confit d'oie Toulousain*, a rich masterpiece of long-simmered goose—a regional specialty from the south of France seldom seen on a New York menu. *Poussin braisé au vinaigre* is another of those French specialties most local restaurants do not prepare correctly. L'Olivier's version of the delicate whole baby chicken in vinegar sauce follows the original Paul Bocuse recipe and does not temper its faint tartness by a sweetening of tomato. The Stendahl Choice here is the *civet de lapin à l'ancienne*. The rabbit is not overly meaty, but each bite is delectable, bathed in a wine sauce that demands to be sopped. Desserts often seem less than adequate, again with that paradoxical exception—*gâteau Turinois*, a double-rich chocolate delight that merits superlatives. The wine list is modest and conceals no bargains. A meal for two with appropriate wines can all too readily escalate to over $50.

L'OLIVIER, 248 East 49th Street, Manhattan. Telephone: (212) 355-1810. Hours: 12-2:30, 6-11, Monday-Friday; 6-11, Saturday; closed Sunday. Cards: AE, DC, MC. Street parking. Reservations suggested. Full bar service.

Sole Anglaise Belle Meunière 13.00

Filet de Bass "L'Olivier" 12.50

Ris de Veau aux Morilles 12.50

Civet de Lapin à l'Ancienne 11.00

Médaillon de Veau Vallée d'Auge 12.50

Noisette d'Agneau à l'Estragon 12.50

Poussin Braisé au Vinaigre 10.50

Caneton Bourguignonne 12.50

Cassoulet Maison 11.00

Confit d'Oie Toulousain 11.00

Entrecôte Sautée au Roquefort 13.50

Steak au Poivre Vert 13.50

Manhattan: Midtown West
LORD (INDIA) RESTAURANT
Indian & Indonesian

$

The Lord giveth good things. One of them is a cozy little restaurant where you can literally dine like a lord on authentic Indian food and pay a pittance for the privilege. Every day there are four complete lunches that range from an easy $2.45 to a comfortable $3.95. This last includes a piece of excellent tandoori broiled chicken, a *shammi kabob* (that's a spicy meat patty), rice pilaf, *dal* (the typical and essential bland lentil purée), a fried vegetable side dish, a small bowl of onion relish, a chutney and coffee or tea. For 50 cents more you can get one of those delicious Indian breads called *paratha.* Nighttime, if you can believe it, you can get a full Indian dinner: appetizers, soup, mild and creamy chicken *masala,* vegetable, *dal,* rice and dessert, plus a beverage, for $5.75. The lavish tandoori dinner featuring the works is only $7.75. In New York! Of course, you can tailor-make a feast à la carte, tossing in any of five Indonesian entrées that the chef makes a specialty of—but don't blame me if your bill comes to a whopping $9 or $10. Best of all, Mohmmad, your polite and gracious host, simply loves to welcome guests and to explain in detail just what each dish is about.

THE LORD (INDIA) RESTAURANT, 102 West 43rd Street, Manhattan. Telephone: (212) 221-6574. Hours: 11:30-11, Monday-Friday; 1-11, Saturday-Sunday. Cards: AE, BA/Visa, CB, DC, MC. Reservations suggested. Street parking. Full bar service.

NASIGORENG,
Spicy Fried Rich Cooked with Chopped Lamb, Chicken and Shrimp 3.95

POR AJAM,
Spiced Chicken Cooked with Pineapple in Coconut Cream 3.95

SAMBAL OEDANG,
Spiced Shrimp Cooked in Coconut Cream   4.25

OPAR DAGING,
Spiced Beef Cooked in Coconut Cream 3.95

TELUR MASAK,
Fried Egg with Spicy Sauce 3.95

TANDOORI CHICKEN,
Chicken Marinated in Yogurt and Mild Spices and Cooked in Oven 5.75

CHICKEN TIKKA,
Boneless Chicken Pieces Marinated and Roasted Tandoori Style 5.75

BOTI KABAB,
Cubed Leg of Lamb Roasted on a Skewer   5.75

SHEEKH KABAB,
Minced Lamb Mixed with Onions and Herbs and Roasted on Skewers 5.75

TANDOORI MIXED GRILL,
An Assortment of Tandoori Specialties 6.75

TANDOORI CHICKEN MASALA,
Tandoori Chicken Cooked with Heavy Cream and Mild Spices 5.75

CHICKEN TIKKA MASALA,
Cooked with Butter and Cream Sauce 5.75

VEGETABLE MADRAS,
Cooked with Tomatoes 3.50

VEGETABLE MASALA 3.50

NAVRATTAN CURRY,
Nine Vegetable Nuts and Mild 3.50

BHINDI MASALA,
Okra, Dry Cooked with Spices 3.75

ALOO PALAK,
Cooked with Potato and Spinac' 3.75

JAL PIAZI,
Cooked with Hot Peppers 3.75

Manhattan: Lower East Side
LUCHOW'S
German $$

Victor Herbert helped to found ASCAP in a back room at Luchow's, Diamond Jim Brady and his gorgeous Lillian Russell dined overlavishly here, and the original owner was responsible for distributing the first Wurzburger beer to New York. Since the days when The Beautiful People were immortals like Paderewski and Caruso, Luchow's has been supplying food to capacity crowds. Little has changed over the generations, except that the moose heads are a bit more moth-eaten and not so many fine beers are on tap in the tin-ceilinged, bare-wood saloon bar. Luchow's has become an endless round of festivals celebrating bock beer, October beer, the Christmas goose, and on and on. Oompah bands make the floor shake, string groups grind out Franz Lehar melodies, and everyone's eyes grow moist when "The tallest indoor Christmas tree in the world" is lit in December. Families, lovers and pinochle players stand in line awaiting their tables. The clash of knives and forks sounds like a small battle as diners stow away giant portions of home-made bratwurst on a bed of tangy sauerkraut, pig's knuckle, sauerbraten, red cabbage, German beer and wines, and wheel-sized German pancakes, lathered with lingonberries and flamed in kirsch. Complete seven-course dinners start at $9.95, but there are plenty of extras and specials higher than that on the extensive menu. A fine choice of German wines is modestly priced. *Prosit*—and pass the bicarb!

LUCHOW'S, 110 East 14th Street, Manhattan. Telephone: (212) 477-4860. Hours: 11:30-10, Monday-Thursday; 12-11, Friday-Saturday; 12-10, Sunday. Cards: AE, BA/Visa, CB, DC, MC. Reservations imperative. Free parking after 6 pm. Full bar service.

SLICED BONELESS BREAST OF GOOSE
EVERY YEAR SINCE 1903
Lüchow's Apple Dressing.
Red Cabbage, Home Fried Potatoes.
14.75

BOILED PLATE OF BEEF
1904, 1959
with Carrots and Horseradish Sauce.
Boiled Potato.
11.75

CORNED PIG'S KNUCKLES
1961
on Sauerkraut with
Whipped-In-Cream Potatoes
11.50

SCHNITZEL A LA LÜCHOW
1902, 1903, 1954

Milk Fed Veal Steak topped with
Champignons and Scrambled Eggs Souffle.
Asparagus Tips Hollandaise.
Lüchow's Roast Potato.
14.50

LÜCHOW'S FAMOUS HOUSE PLATTER
1905, 1928, 1968

Boiled Baked Beef, Bratwurst, Bauernwurst,
and Knackwurst in Vegetable Jardinière
or Saurkraut. Duchesse Potatoes
(For 2) 12.50 per person

Manhattan: Midtown East
LUTECE
French
$$$

Lutece (the ancient name for Paris) nestles in a narrow two-story brownstone. Downstairs there is an enclosed garden, but I prefer the naturalness of the comfortable upstairs rooms. The reputation of Lutece is high, and with justification. Finesse is in everything they do, in service, in decor and in cuisine, with emphasis always on a lovely presentation. (I like restaurants that are proud enough of their offerings to display them to the table before serving.) I cannot quite agree with those who acclaim Lutece as New York's number-one restaurant, but it is certainly among the top two or three. Almost everything here, from hors d'oeuvre and potages through main dishes and desserts, is outstanding. A specialty of the house is *mignon de boeuf en croûte Lutece,* a serving of first-rate beef, pink and tender, individually encased in a fine puff pastry, with a winey mushroom duxelle layered in between. On some occasions there is a similar fine pastry-case treatment of lamb or chicken. The wine list is a fine one, with selections personally made by chef-proprietor Andre Soltner. They are, however, often "officially" out of some wines that other diners are able to get a day later—this smacks of favoritism. One other annoyance—only the person suspected of being the host receives a menu with prices. And what are those concealed prices? Take it for granted that you will be enjoying one of the most expensive meals in New York. Though totally irrelevant, I cannot think of Lutece without recalling that M. Soltner, on his summer trips back to France, is rumored to bring his family American chocolate bars and peanut butter!

LUTECE, 249 East 50th Street, Manhattan. Telephone: (212) PL2-2225. Hours: 12-2, 6-9:45, Monday-Friday; 6-9:45 Saturday; closed Sunday. Cards: AE. Reservations required. Street parking. Full bar service.

Manhattan: Greenwich Village
MAIN STREET
American

$$

Contrary to popular belief, there is an American cuisine, one that began with English, Dutch and French settlers. This is the worthy concept of Main Street. While the food has its ups and downs, the professed aim here is self-improvement: They even request patrons to submit their own regional recipes. For example, they introduced a New Orleans sandwich called a Peacemaker, made with fried oysters baked right into a small loaf of bread. One customer stated that in *his* family, the Peacemaker was always served with a little cup of fish broth. Done. Then another customer said he was delighted with the authenticity of the sandwich, but why didn't the broth have tomato bits floating in it. Done again. There is a whole booklet of rotating menus. Tuesday, however, is not always New England Day, so you take potluck (a good American tradition) unless you phone ahead to check which region is being featured. A few examples: New England, maple baked acorn squash; South, Brunswick stew and Creole jambalaya; Midwest, "snibbled" green beans tossed with bacon; Far West, "Frisco" *cioppino.* A Southwestern Zuni lamb stew with juniper berries and green chili oddly needs more spice. The Stendahl Choice here is barbecued beef ribs in a tantalizing sweet and smoky, mustardy red sauce. Corn sticks and buttermilk biscuits are provided. The apple brown Betty needs a crunchier crumb crust, but the chocolate cake is a dream. Service is friendly, decor is fascinatingly original, and the list of California wines is masterfully chosen. Lunch and brunches are about $5; dinners about $14.

MAIN STREET, 75 Greenwich Avenue, Manhattan. Telephone: (212) 929-1579. Hours: 12-4, 6-11:30, Sunday-Friday; until 1 am, Saturday; closed Monday. Cards: AE, BA/Visa, DC, MC. Reservations suggested. Street parking. Full bar service.

Manhattan: Midtown East
MADRAS WOODLANDS
Southern Indian

$

Madras Woodlands specializes exclusively in vegetarian foods. But if you were not told, you would scarcely know you were eating a meatless, fishless, eggless dinner, such is the culinary magic at this little restaurant. I have been in Madras, and further south, but never have I tasted food of this sort served with such unobtrusive hospitality as at Madras Woodlands. Decor is romantic, with low lighting, crimson trimmings and handsome murals. One extraordinary feature is the Thali special (lunch or dinner, only $4.95). On the table appears a great covered silver disc. When the lid is lifted, you behold a neatly folded whole wheat chapati and silver bowls containing *rasam, sambar, poriyal, dhal kotto, pachidi, pappadum* and yoghurt. No matter what the dishes are named, you must be a Southern Indian to identify which is which. The Thali—and other dishes too—are all made of vegetables, with sauces hot and mild, served in individual bowls. Vegetables? Yes, but disguised as bubbly little pancakes, crispy fritters, crunchy doughnuts or miniature stews in zestful sauces scented with coriander, turmeric and other curry-type spices. The pancakes come plain, or topped or filled with such things as potato, onion and nuts—you won't miss the meat. A complete dinner may be had for $4.95 up to $7.95. There is an inexpensive wine list, but with this perky sort of food, beer goes best.

MADRAS WOODLANDS, 310 East 44th Street. Manhattan. Telephone: (212) 986-0620. Hours: 12-2:30, 5:30-10:30, Monday-Friday; 1-10:30, Saturday-Sunday. Cards: AE, BA/Visa, CB, DC, MC. Reservations recommended. Street parking. Full bar service.

Specialities

PLAIN PAPER DOSAI	1.95
Very thin crepes	
MASALA DOSAI	2.25
Crepes filled with potato, onion, nuts	
RAVA DOSAI	1.95
Wheat crepes	
SPECIAL RAVA DOSAI	2.25
Wheat crepes with onions	
UTHAPPAM	1.95
a la lentil pancakes	
VEGETABLE UTHAPPAM	2.45
Onion/tomato/peas pancakes	
SPECIAL OMELETTE	2.45
Served with sauce (2)	
SPECIAL RICE or UPPUMA	2.25
With Sambhar Curry	
POORIS & VEGETABLE CURRY	2.25

Lunch

EXPRESS LUNCH	2.95
Special rice, sambar, vegetable curry pickles, chutney, papad & coffee	
MADRAS LUNCH	3.95
Iddly or Medhu Vadai or Special Vegetable Vadai or Bajjis PLUS Masala Dosai or Special Rava Dosai or Vegetable Uthappam PLUS tea or coffee	
THALI	4.95
7 Course Entree, rasam, sambar, poriyal, dhal pachidi, papad & special rice, tea or coffee	

HOT CHUTNEY/MELKAI PODI/YOGURT/SAMBAR/
   Any extra items from Thali   0.60

Manhattan: Upper East Side
MAXWELL'S PLUM
Continental $$

Here is a Mack Sennett version of Maxim's of Paris—a three-ring circus unlike any place else in New York. No put-down; I like it that way. There are three separate menus with food that varies from a light supper snack for $2.95 through a Cafe Dinner ($4.75-$14.85) to a Back Room Dinner ($6.45-$14.85). And in between there are plenty of à la carte extras to fatten the check. There are also three separate sections of the restaurant: Down front is a bar often packed three-deep with singles, doubles and the ambisextrous, with possibly a dazed tourist jimmied between. Along the sides is the Cafe, which resembles an overcrowded porch. Above is the Back Room that takes off from Maxim's with a colorful ceiling of stained glass. And everywhere there is art deco, Tiffany glass, nudie statues, stuffed or painted objects, green growing things, pink or lavender non-growing things, and if-you-can-name-it-you-can-find-it things. The singles-shambles down front might discourage a serious diner, but the Back Room serves food that is the equal of many a haughty *haute cuisine* establishment. Hamburgers and chili bowls may be tucked between whiskey sours at the bar, but beneath the illuminated stained-glass ceiling you can begin with *celeri remoulade* with spiced beets, tomato and onion; lobster, avocado and pineapple à la Russe; Iranian golden caviar with blinis; or fish soup with *rouille*, the great chili-garlic mayonnaise of Provence. Main dishes range from pastas through fish, lamb, beef or exotics such as venison and sometimes wild boar, to curries, Oriental-style spareribs, or German sausages.

MAXWELL'S PLUM, 64th Street and First Avenue, Manhattan. Telephone: (212) 628-2100. Hours: 12-2 am, Monday-Saturday; 12-11, Sunday. Cards: AE, BA/Visa, CB, DC, MC. Reservations recommended. Parking in nearby garages. Full bar service.

Manhattan: Midtown West
MAYOOR
Indian $

Mayoor means peacock, and this restaurant has a beautiful one in full plumage—an impressive metal sculpture handsomely backlighted in a wall niche. Despite its striking, though understated, decor and good food, Mayoor does not seem to attract the clientele it deserves. Perhaps this is due to its location on a "restaurant row" of more prosaic French and Italian restaurants. The large square dining room is papered with regal blue raw silk, and on each table there are large bubble glasses that blossom with suavely folded linen napkins. Diners who fear spicy foods should know that Mayoor specializes in Moghlai cooking, which is among the subtlest of Indian cuisines. (The Moghuls were princes who once rode on the backs of diamond-studded elephants, and they could afford the most refined cooking possible.) This subtle food and the romantic ambience are available at gorgeously low prices. Complete luncheons are $4.95; dinners are $7.95 and $8.95. À la carte meals will run above the $10 mark, but are worth exploring. The Stendahl Choice is the Indian specialty, *pomfret*. Even though this rare fish has to be flown over frozen, it tastes like the freshest of finny things after it has been marinated in yoghurt and spices and sizzled in the tandoor oven. Lamb and chicken may be had here as *pasanda* and *murgh mussallam*, both in velvet sauces that are faintly aromatic but as suave as a Raj. The wine list is low priced, but limited. Better choices are coffee, tea or beer.

MAYOOR, 37 West 56th Street, Manhattan. Telephone: (212) 757-3939. Hours: 12-11, Monday-Friday; 5:30-11, Saturday; closed Sunday. Cards: AE, BA/Visa, DC, MC. Reservations suggested. Parking in nearby garage. Full bar service.

Manhattan: Greenwich Village
MEXI-FROST (DELICIAS MEJICANAS)
Mexican $

Although they have knocked down a wall to expand the number of tables from six to 10, and although they are trying to change the name from Mexi-Frost to the rather snooty Delicias Mejicanas, this is still one of the great places for Mexican food in New York. Everything—even the tortillas—is freshly made in the miniature kitchen. What I especially like about Mexi-Frost (and if the microscopic awning still calls it that, so can I) is its purity. Paper mats are always fresh, paper napkins are plentifully supplied, and clean glasses will be proffered to hold the beer and wine you bring yourself. You know you are in for real Mexican food the minute you dip a freshly crisped tortilla chip into the table hot sauce. Red, rich, thick, with a tongue-tickling piquancy, it is possibly the most authentic hot sauce in town. The nachos are the precisely correct mix of bland beans and cheese buttered on a tortilla chip, prettily adorned with a ring of fiery jalapeño pepper. There are a few interesting Spanish and Latin combinations, but Mexi-Frost's fame and fortune have been made on their Mexican combinations. The tortillas are soft, the cheese is right, the sauce likewise, and the food comes to your table sizzling on metal platters. What more could a lucky gringo ask? Only a few things: The beans and rice are not as good as they used to be and the overly thick batter on the *chile relleno con queso* deprives the cheese-stuffed green chile of some of its piquancy. A robust meal here will set you back $5 to $7.

MEXI-FROST (DELICIAS MEJICANAS), 220 West 13th Street, Manhattan. Telephone: (212) CH2-9389. Hours: 11-10:30, Monday-Thursday; 3-11, Friday-Sunday. No credit cards. Reservations not accepted. Street parking. No bar service; bring your own beer or wine.

MEXICAN COMBINATIONS

all combinations served with rice & beans
choice of BEEF CHICKEN CHORIZO
CHEESE ENCHILADA .50¢ EXTRA

# 1	TACO TAMAL ENCHILADA	$4.25
# 2	TACO ENCHILADA TOSTADA	4.25
# 3	TACO TAMAL EMPANADA	4.25
# 4	ENCHILADA TAMAL EMPANADA	4.25
# 5	EMPANADA ENCHILADA	3.35
# 6	TAMAL ENCHILADA	3.35
# 7	TACO ENCHILADA	3.35
# 8	TOSTADA ENCHILADA	3.35

ESPECIALIDADES DEL CHEF

 # 9 FROM NORTHERN SPAIN (GALICIA)
ARROZ CON POLLO, CAMARONES Y CHORIZO
VALENCIA RICE COOKED ON AN OPEN FLAME IN A MIXTURE OF YOUNG TENDER CHICKEN PARTS, SHRIMP HAM AND SAUSAGES 4.65

 # 10 FROM ARGENTINA
BEEFSTEAK DE BAHIA BLANCA
SHELL STEAK GRILLED CAREFULLY TO PERFECTION, THE ARGENTINE WAY. BASTED WITH A SPECIAL SAUCE, "CHIMI CHURRI" SERVED WITH A FRESH SALAD 4.95

 # 11 "MEXICO"
ENCHILADAS SUIZAS OUR OWN HOME MADE TORTILLAS FILLED WITH TENDER PIECES OF CHICKEN AND COVERED WITH A DELICIOUS GREEN SAUCE IS TOPPED WITH SOUR CREAM AND BAKED TO PERFECTION, SALADE, RICE AND BEANS ARE INCLUDED. 4.95

 # 12 "ECUADOR"
YAPINGACHOS FROM THE ANDES OF ECUADOR YAPINGACHOS ARE POTATOES FILLED WITH CHEESE PAN FRIED TO A CRISP DELIGHT AND TOPPED WITH A SAUCE CREATED CENTURIES AGO BY THE INCAS. FINALLY THIS DISH IS COVERED WITH A FRIED EGG AND SERVED ON A BED OF LETTUCE AND AVOCADO 4.25

 # 13 "PERU"
ANTICUCHOS FROM THE INCAS OF PERU COMES THE SHISH KABOB OF SOUTH AMERICA. RICE AND BEANS INCLUDED 3.95

Manhattan: Lower Midtown East
MR. LEE'S
International

$$$

If you long to recapture those sunny memories of patio dining along Mediterranean shores, visit Mr. Lee's. Though forbiddingly closed-looking from without, the interior radiates a cheerful aura with green plants, glowing skylight, pretty flowers and glistening wine glasses. Mr. Lee, a charming raconteur and world traveler from Hong Kong, is your host. Mrs. Lee does the cooking, presenting European classics subtly transformed by a delicate Oriental touch. Warm bread, twisted sesame-seed pretzels born of the Middle East, begins your adventure. Appetizers include European specialties and a Chinese spring roll as light as French pastry. A soup follows, perhaps an ethereal cold avocado or a hot cream of asparagus, exquisitely light and exotic with an Oriental touch of crunchy asparagus tips. The Stendahl Choice among the entrées is a piquant bass with bananas, flamed in cognac, a combination that tastes far better than it may sound. There is also pigeon, tinged with soy; a spicy steak *au poivre;* and an unusual, very delicate lemon chicken. Desserts are as exotic as the main dishes. Most entrées on the à la carte dinner menu are $12 and up, but are several dollars less at luncheon. The lunch menu also features some uncommon egg dishes such as eggs Portuguese, poached eggs atop chopped tomato in a puff paste shell, topped with an airy hollandaise. There are no bargains on the wine list, but Mr. Lee's very personal choices are guarantees of good bibbing. At night an 18 percent service is built into the check.

MR. LEE'S, 337 Third Avenue, Manhattan. Telephone: (212) MU9-6373. Hours: 12-3, 6-11, Monday-Friday; 6-11, Saturday; closed Sunday. Cards: AE, BA/Visa, DC, MC. Reservations suggested. Parking in nearby garage. Full bar service.

Sole Meuniere	12.50
Scampi Maison	12.00
Shrimps Lobster Sauce	12.00
Shrimp Curry	12.00
Bar Poché au Beurre Blanc	12.00
Chicken Florentine	12.50
Veal Picata	13.50
Pigeon à La Façon du Chef	10.00
Chicken Kiev	10.75
Chicken Wellington	12.50
Mignon de Boeuf Wellington (2)	30.00
Chateaubriand (2)	28.00
Entrecote Nature	14.50
Tournedos Rossini	14.50
Steak au Poivre	16.75
Lemon Chicken	12.00
Canard aux Kumquats	16.00
Banana Bass	12.80
Bouillabaisse	16.00
Lobster Sole Cardinal	19.50

Manhattan: Midtown East
MONSIGNORE II
Italian $$

Monsignore II, a phoenix that rose from the ashes of a fire that destroyed Monsignore I, outshines its predecessor. It is a handsome establishment: coral-colored walls lined with glossy murals painted on aluminum panels. There are many unusual dishes on the menu; captains and waiters are suave. Even the carafe wine is a heady Drepano from Sicily, not an ordinary Soave or Bardolino. The only fault is that the wine list carries other rare beauties, not to be found in the cellar. However, many popular Italian and French wines are around $9 a bottle. Always ask about the specials of the day; they are imaginative and always beautifully prepared. Stendahl's Choice for pasta here is *bimbollotti alla Monsignore*. The pasta itself varies, including shells, ditali, or small ziti, but the heavenly sauce is constant—cream, mushrooms, peas and ham. This is served al dente; a similar baked version is fettuccine Jessica. On my first visit, waiters and captains knew at once what *arriabata* was, although not

Pesce

Mazzancolli alla Moda del Chef	9.75
Scampi in the Mode of the Chef	
Zuppa di Pesce Melodia del Golfo di Napoli	10.75
Stew of Fish and Seafood in Special Broth	
Sogliola-Garcita O'Sole Mio	9.75
Stuffed Sole with Lobster and Crabmeat	
Branzino alla Livornese	9.75
Striped Bass Sauteed with Wine, Tomato	
Branzino alla Griglia	9.75
Broiled Striped Bass	

Carni

Osso Buco con Risotto Milanese	9.75
Scallopine di Maiale Pizzaiola	9.75
Sliced Filet of Pork with Tomato, Garlic, Parsley	
Cotoletta di Vitello Fontina	9.75
Sauteed Veal Cutlet with Prosciutto, Fontina Cheese	

many New York Italian establishments do. They brought forth an impeccable pasta dressed with this Sicilian "enraged" sauce, authentically spicy. Characteristic of Monsignore's meat sauces is a definite hand with the seasonings and a light hand with the thickening. A decided plus is the way vegetables are treated. A *vitello Fontina* came on one occasion with French peas and scalloped potatoes flecked with pimientos; another time the same dish came with a potato patty and zucchini crusted with cheese. Both *baccalao* or *bass alla Livornese* are excellent, the fish succulent and dressed with a pair of mussels, tomatoes, black olives and green peppers in wine. Desserts rate a fabulous. I counted nine, ranging from a homemade Napoleon to a pineapple *zuppa inglese.* The bill for lunch here will average $10, dinner $15.

MONSIGNORE II, 61 East 55th Street, Manhattan. Telephone: (212) 355-2070. Hours: 12-3, 5:30-12, Monday-Friday; 5:30-12, Saturday; closed Sunday. Cards: AE, BA/Visa, CB, DC, MC. Reservations suggested. Valet parking. Full bar service.

Scaloppine di Vitello King Alfonso *Slices of Veal Sauteed with Tomatoes, Shallots, Mushrooms*	9.75
Vitello alla Sorrentina *Breaded Veal Scallop with Eggplant, Cheese Tomato*	9.75
Piccata di Vitello *Sauteed Slices of Veal with Lemon*	9.75
Suprema di Pollo alla Tiberio *Breaded Breast of Chicken Stuffed with Veal and Sausage*	9.75
Pollo alla Marengo *Braised Chicken with Tomato, Olives, Mushrooms, Brandy*	9.75
Petto di Pollo all'Alba *Breast of Chicken with Truffles, Fontina Cheese*	9.75
Gegato alla Veneziana *Calf's Liver with Onions*	9.75
Saltimbocca di Casa *Sauteed Slices of Veal with Broccoli Fontina*	9.75
Vera Fiorentina ai Ferri *Broiled Sirloin Steak*	12.75
Gianco di Bue Salsa ai Funghi *London Broil, Sauce Bordelaise*	9.75
Costolette di Abbacchio Scottadito *Rack of Lamb - Roman Style*	12.75

Manhattan: Upper West Side
MOON PALACE
Chinese $

Even though Moon Palace is far from Chinatown, many Chinese families can be seen dining here, always a sign of a reliable chef. There is no glamor to Moon Palace beyond its poetic name. It is a huge, somewhat barren place, totally functional, without fuss and certainly no feathers. Yet the atmosphere is pleasant—and it conceals a menu of gold. Also, the waiters, despite an occasional difficulty with English, are alert and helpful. The menu includes cooking from many regions of China, but the kitchen excels in the dishes of Peking. The classic Peking duck is a good buy here at only $14; with its eight thin pancakes, it makes a fine basis for a dinner for six to eight. Dumplings, steamed, boiled or fried, are all first-rate. A Stendahl Choice is the dish known as chicken with pork in two styles. This is a platter made up of tender white shreds of chicken in a light sauce and pork shreds in a darker, spicy sauce, the two meats separated by a strip of lightly cooked spinach. Combination lunches start at $2.40, dinners at only $3. But for range and adventure, it is far better to order à la carte. As a footnote: Some time ago, during a lobster shortage, Moon Palace added 25 cents to each lobster dish. Just as soon as the shortage was over, they took off that 25 cents. That's the splendid kind of restaurant that Moon Palace is.

MOON PALACE, 2879 Broadway, Manhattan. Telephone: (212) 666-7517. Hours: 11:30-10, Sunday-Thursday; until 11, Friday-Saturday. No credit cards. Reservations not necessary. Street parking. Full bar service.

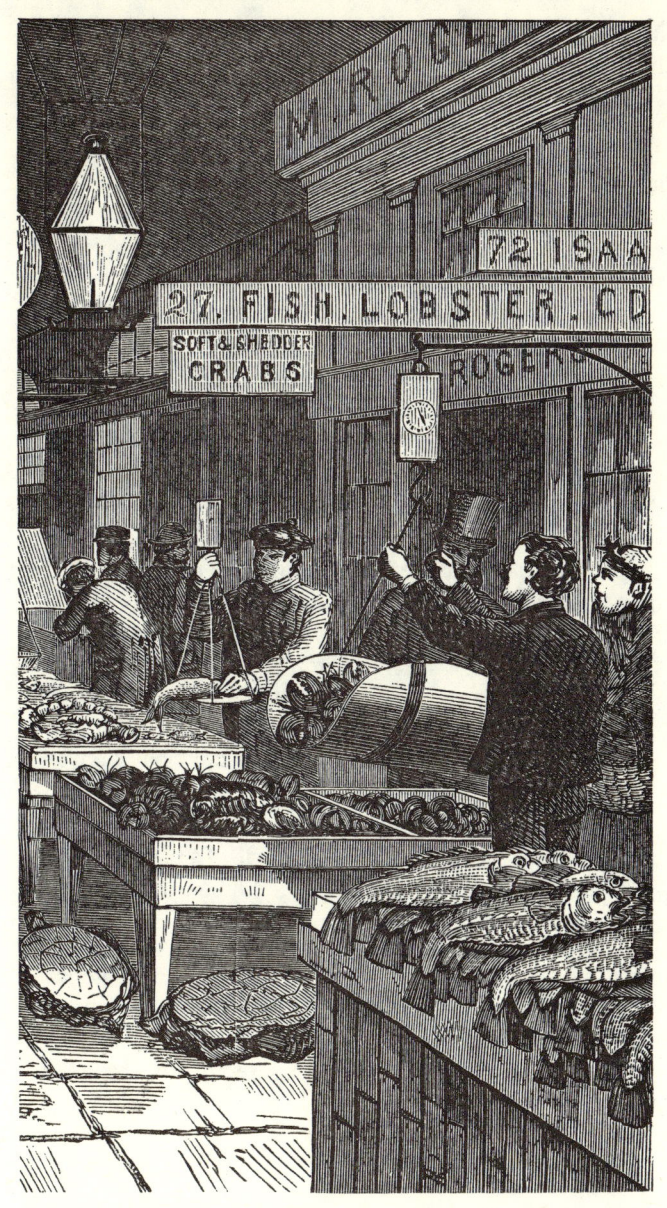

Fulton Fish Market, 1869.

Manhattan: Midtown East
NIPPON
Japanese

$$

Japanese restaurants have proliferated like dandelions in the last few years. Many are good, a few fine, and their food ranges from some of the cheapest to some of the most expensive in the city. Nippon has always struck me as more truly Japanese than most. Its warm-lit, beige aura, its long bar (an artistic creation made of white wood imported from Japan), the skill of its sashimi and sushi chefs, and the aristocratic bearing of its waitresses make Nippon seem like a regal establishment in old Kyoto. Because of a family connection they also serve the best saki in New York. Most sakis we get here are purposely made a bit sweet for American tastes; Nippon's unique brand is dry. Ask for *Aramasa*. As far as I am aware there is nothing else here that one cannot find at other fine Japanese restaurants. It is only that the fish seems just a shade fresher, more tender; the tempura a microscopic bit more greaseless, the dipping sauces a mite more delicate. From a seat at the bar, you watch the chefs make sashimi or sushi. At the neat small tables or in one of the tatami rooms, your butterfly waitress will serve complete meals. The tempura or sukiyaki dinners are priced around $10. There is a special O-Teishoku dinner at $12 and a still more super Omakase dinner, the classic Japanese fish feast at $20 to $30. The large number of Japanese customers indicates that Nippon is doing a lot of things right.

NIPPON, 145 East 52nd Street, Manhattan. Telephone: (212) EL5-9020. Lunch: 12-2:30, Monday-Friday. Dinner: 5:30-10, Monday-Thursday; until 10:30, Friday-Saturday; closed Sunday. Cards: AE, DC, MC. Reservations required. Street parking. Full bar service.

Luncheon

O-Teishoku

Includes consomme or soy bean soup, pickled vegetables, rice and desserts.

1. *Tempura*

Assorted tidbits of seafood and vegetables, gently fried with a uniquely delicate batter in sesame oil.

2. *Gyunikunabe*

A distinctive ragout prepared at your own table with Japanese white wine, bamboo shoots and other exotic ingredients.

3. *Shioyaki*

Fresh fish broiled with salts served with unique Japanese sauce.

4. *Sashimi*

Filet of thinly sliced fresh raw fish served with ginger and a piquant soy sauce.

5. *Tonkatsu*

Deep fried pork filet.

6. *Sushi*

A famous traditional delicacy—thin slices of fresh raw fish, served with ginger and piquant soy sauce.

7. *O-Teishoku*

Traditional Japanese meal, a combination of four entrees of the day.

Manhattan: Midtown West
NIRVANA ON ROOFTOP
Indian $

You get to Nirvana by an elevator, but the proper means of locomotion should be a magic carpet, for you fly up to a penthouse that overlooks Central Park. And there is a wall-long mirror to reflect its green beauty even when you sit with your back to the window. That's only one bit of magic. The whole interior of Nirvana is decorated with turmeric-colored cloth sparkling with tiny mirrors. Intricately carved screens hide little cubicles for the most private dining in Manhattan. At night, Indian musicians tootle seductively to create aural incense. Most lunches are under $5, and dinners under $10, so you can afford to add a few exotic tidbits from the list of side dishes and made-to-order breads. For me, these intriguing snacks are the best part of the menu, and most cost under $1. They include *roti,* flat whole wheat bread toasted without butter on a grill; *parata,* multi-layered bread fried lightly in butter; and *keema parata,* bread stuffed with curried ground meat. This last is almost a meal in itself. Best is the fascinating *poori,* a giant dough balloon big as a volleyball—which, when pulled apart, collapses into warm pastry flakes. A Stendahl Choice. There are 18 curries to choose from, plus *biryanis* (pilafs) and other dishes. Fresh coriander chutney is a tangy must. There is a moderately priced wine list, but beer is best. Or on a hot summer day try a *lassi,* a suave cooler of yoghurt and rose water.

NIRVANA, 30 Central Park South, Manhattan. Telephone: (212) 752-0270. Hours: 12-12, Sunday-Thursday, until 1 am, Friday-Saturday. No credit cards. Reservations suggested. Valet parking. Full bar service.

BHUNA GOSHT curried meat chunks pan broiled till sauces absorbed (made to order, medium spicy, hot or very hot)

BEEF	6.95
LAMB	6.95

CURRY well cooked with sauce of intricately blended spices in the age old tradition of India (made to order medium spicy, hot or very hot)

BEEF	5.95
BEEF (COOKED WITH FRESH CABBAGE)	5.95
BRAIN (LAMB)	5.95
CHICKEN	5.95
DUCK	7.95
EGGS OF SWEET WATER FISH	7.95
FISH (FRESH SWEET WATER FISH)	5.95
GOAT MEAT (COOKED WITH A FRESH VEGETABLE)	5.95
KEEMA (GROUND MEAT)	5.95
LAMB	5.95
LAMB (COOKED WITH SPINACH)	6.95
LOBSTER	7.95
SHRIMP (COOKED WITH A FRESH VEGETABLE)	7.95
SHRIMP MALAI (COOKED WITH COCONUT MILK)	7.95
SUN DRIED FISH (COOKED WITH FRESH VEGETABLES)	5.95
VEGETABLE BHAJI (FRESHLY FRIED DRY MIXED VEGETABLES)	4.95
VEGETABLE (FRESH MIXED VEGETABLES)	3.95

KORMA similar to curry but very mild cooked with ghee, yogurt and mildly spiced sauce

CHICKEN	6.95
FISH (FRESH SWEET WATER FISH)	6.95

Manhattan: Midtown West
ORSINI'S
Northern Italian $$$

Despite its being an "in" place for society's pets, Orsini's is always warmly welcoming to "just plain folks" like us. This has always impressed me. Downstairs, where only dinner is served, the ambience is candlelit baroque. But I prefer sitting upstairs, particularly when sunlight streams in to create an effect of garden dining in sunny Tuscany. If you are not a jet setter, you may not get the very best table, but you will generally get a good one, and you will be served as if you were a celebrity. You will also pay stiff prices for all this courteous service and fine food. *Mozzarella in carrozza* (molten cheese in a "carriage" of toast) is one of the better versions, as it should be at $4.25. Soups are heartily satisfying, which proves Beautiful People like earthy potages, too. Pastas are most carefully prepared here, and when they have *fettuccine al porcino,* with imported wild mushrooms from northern Italy, it is worth its

Farinacei

Fettuccine Alfredo 8.50
(egg noodles, butter sauce as in Rome)

Tortellini Alla Panna 8.50
(dumplings filled with chicken meat; butter & cream sauce)

Linguine alle Vongole 8.50
(with white or red clam sauce)

Cannelloni 8.50
(large noodles filled with meat sauce)

Spaghettini alla Chitarra 8.50
(great sauce; peas, prosciutto and mushrooms)

Fettuccine Capri 9.00
(a new sauce, ask us)

Rigatoni alla Baronessa 8.50
(sauce made of tomatoes, fresh mushrooms and chicken livers)

Crespelle alla Fiorentina 9.00
(delicate crêpes filled with spinach, prosciutto & bechamel)

bitter $12 cost. *Pollo all' arrabbiata* (misnamed as being from Rome when true *arrabbiata,* "enraged sauce," is a Sicilian classic) is good, but I prefer *pollo scarpariello,* boneless chicken "shoemaker" style, enlivened with white wine, mushrooms and black olives. My choice among the veal dishes is *cuscinetti di vitello,* light morsels of veal, enriched with prosciutto and Gruyère. Often the rooms ring with the sound of whisks beating against copper bowls in the creation of *zabaglione al Marsala,* but my preference in desserts goes to the zesty and rich *zuppa inglese.* Wines are well chosen and not overpriced. I do resent the sneaky cover charge of 75 cents per person for bread and butter. At Orsini prices they could afford to give you a bag of bread to take home, gratis. Luncheons average about $12; dinners well above $20.

ORSINI'S, 41 West 56th Street, Manhattan. Telephone: (212) PL7-1698. Hours: 12-3, 5:30-1, Monday-Saturday; closed Sunday. Cards: AE, CB, DC, MC. Reservations suggested. Parking in nearby garage. Full bar service.

Piatti del Giorno

Cuscinetti di Vitello 12.50
(pillows of veal; prosciutto, gruyere cheese, wine sauce)

Mignonette Peperonata 11.50
(sliced filet mignon with peppers and spiced tomato sauce)

Cotoletta alla Milanese 9.50
(breaded veal cutlet)

Fegato alla Veneziana 9.50
(calf liver, venetian style)

Pollo all' Arrabbiata 9.00
(recipe from Rome; chicken white wine sauce)

Piccata al Limone 9.25
(veal, lemon and butter sauce)

Vitello alla Sorrentina 9.50
(veal, mozzarella cheese, eggplant, wine sauce)

Manhattan: Midtown East
OYSTER BAR & RESTAURANT
Seafood $

Fish lovers jam this historic institution, buried on the lower level of Grand Central Station. The Oyster Bar specializes in fish from the "top of the catch," the freshest fish on the boat. The menu boasts perhaps the widest choice of finny items available in New York, including all the favorites and rare selections besides: nine types of oysters when in season, ling, tile fish, Florida red grouper, Carolina sturgeon and mako shark. Specials often include *solianka* (Russian sturgeon stew), *waterzoï* (Belgian fish stew), bouillabaisse and its San Francisco/Portuguese cousin, *cioppino*. There is also a full shore dinner that includes clam chowder, steamers with broth, a whole lobster, French fries, hot biscuits, pie and beverage, at only $12.45. What many regulars never suspect is that desserts at the Oyster Bar, made by a pair of Swiss pastry makers, are something special. These include a superior chocolate truffle cake, fresh fruit tarts, orange liqueur pie and daily surprises. The wine list is a breathtaking compendium of more than 60 American wines (no others represented), selected and updated regularly by New York wine-savant Harold Bearak. Among my favorites is a Callaway White Riesling at $9.45. Meals generally range from about $5 to $11. *Important note:* At lunch, devotees pack the place, but after 7 pm, one may dine in almost solitary comfort.

OYSTER BAR & RESTAURANT, Grand Central Station, Manhattan. Telephone: (212) 532-3888. Hours: 11:30-9:30; Monday-Friday; closed Saturday-Sunday. Cards: AE, BA/Visa, CB, DC. Reservations suggested. Parking garage nearby. Full bar service.

TODAY'S CATCH

ITEMS BELOW ARE BROILED, UNLESS INDICATED

BLUEFISH FILET CAROLINA	6.35
BROOK TROUT	
CATFISH FILET MARYLAND FRIED	5.55
FLOUNDER WHOLE PROVINCETOWN	6.65
FINNAN HADDIE STEAMED	7.95
GOLDEYE, LAKE WINNIPEG	
GROUPER FILET FLORIDA	8.15
HADDOCK	
HALIBUT FILET CHATHAM	9.95
LING	
MACKEREL	
PERCH	
POMPANO	
PORGY	
RED SNAPPER	
SALMON, COLUMBIA RIVER KING	10.35
SCALLOPS, BAY FRIED	8.75
SCALLOPS, SEA	
SCROD FILET BOSTON	6.95
SEA BASS	
SHAD 7.55 AND/OR ROE	
SHARK, MAKO STEAK	5.95
SMELTS CANADIAN FRIED	5.95
SOLE FILET LEMON	8.95
SQUID FRIED	5.25
STRIPED BASS	8.95
STURGEON STEAK CAROLINA	8.45
SWORDFISH STEAK	10.75
TILE FISH STEAK	6.95
VIRGINIA SPOTS	
WEAKFISH	
WHITING WHOLE	5.15

Manhattan: Midtown East
THE PALACE
French $$$$

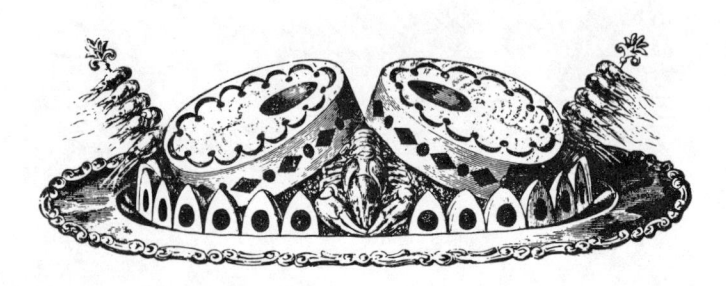

What do you think a perfect meal is worth in dollars? Whatever your answer, the most expensive restaurant in New York has set a price for what they ardently claim to be the finest meal on earth. The basic price is $65 a person, but with the proper wines that such a meal requires, prepare yourself to pay at least $125 per person. A perfect meal, of course, goes beyond mere vittles and the blood of the grape, and that is precisely where The Palace shines— service and ambience are exquisite. The owner argues that people save up to splurge on a wonderful weekend or an operatic orgy; why not squirrel away enough folding money to indulge in an unforgettable dining experience? What can you expect for your $125? Wine that is poured into sparkling cut crystal. Silver candelabra that glow with tall, non-drip tapers. Being surrounded by more solicitous waiters than you need. And even though they are crisply tuxedoed, they are not aloof, but charming and sometimes witty attendants at a ritual. I am happy to report that they do not affect the dreadful pretension of white gloves. The ambience is that of a French manor house, with glimmering chandeliers, light glowing on creamy walls, tables that radiate a pristine gleam. From appetizers through potage, main course, salad and desserts, your meal appears on silver salvers, garnished and decorated to look as lovely as a series of still lifes. Duckling and meats are prepared beyond criticism. The Stendahl Choice, however, is the swordfish. This is sliced as a massive, inch-thick disc of the freshest swordfish center-cut and cooked under intense heat so that it emerges crusty on the outside and moist—even a bit pink—at its heart. Sublime. Desserts and coffee are equally superb, and there are rare cognacs and antique ports for those who wish for the ultimate. Is all this worth $125? Save up your cash and you be the judge.

Footnote: I fault The Palace for its $5 charge for a simple highball, and I think it is an insult that the *service compris* is an automatic 23 percent. I admire the continental way of building the gratuities into *l'addition,* but the traditional 15 percent is enough. Anything over that is the diner's prerogative, not the management's.

THE PALACE, 420 East 59th Street, Manhattan. Telephone: (212) 355-5150. Hours: dinner only, Monday-Saturday; closed Sunday. Cards: AE, BA/Visa. Reservations imperative. Street parking. Full bar service.

Manhattan: Midtown East
PALM TOO
Steakhouse

$$$

Many swear there is only one great steakhouse in New York: The Palm. Others are beginning to swear by another steakhouse: Palm Too. Palm Too is sonny-boy to the original—not a different restaurant, simply an annex across the street from the first. Food, prices, ambience are identical. Habitués of Palm Too do not question the identical quality of the food: "Either place you ask for a black and blue steak, you get it. Anything you order, you get exactly the way you ask for it. And it's the best." But I prefer Palm Too because the waiters don't tread on your feet as much, or jostle as much, and because the Palm Too crowd (and it's always a crowd) seems less noisy and more relaxed. Palm Too has the same Second Avenue twenties look of its sire: sawdust on the floor, beige walls plastered with caricatures and cartoon drawings of sports and advertising agency "stars," plain tables, mostly for twos, and waiters who seem a bit aloof yet who pop food on the table with precise timing. And no menus: Just order what you want and expect to pay a lot. Drinks are potent and filled to the brim. So are the plates of meat and 'taters. You pay stiff prices for every item: steaks are $13. Side orders are enough for four, and include crusty old-style hash browns or fat French fries, or simple, (but excellent) spinach. The fried onions are unusual—crisp golden strawlike threads. Fortunately, almost anything can be had by the half order. Italian specialties and juicy four-pound lobsters are also popular. Most customers are stuffed before dessert time, but there is a custardy *zuppa inglese* and a spectacular chocolate cappuccino pie well worth saving room for.

PALM TOO, 840 Second Avenue, Manhattan. Telephone: (212) 697-5198. Hours: 12-11, Monday-Friday; 5-11, Saturday; closed Sunday. Cards: AE, BA/Visa, CB, DC. Reservations necessary for lunch. Valet parking. Full bar service.

Foot of Broadway, 1831.

Manhattan: Midtown West
THE PARKWAY
Roumanian-Jewish $$

Ordinary standards of dining do not apply to The Parkway. Roumanian-Jewish cooking, while not in this case kosher, is governed by tradition. Because of the way beef must be butchered and cut, a typical Roumanian broiling, to my taste, is chewy and lacks juiciness. My colleagues, however, who remember from childhood weekend feasts featuring such broilings, insist that The Parkway is perfect. There are the delicacies known as unborn eggs, and *schmaltz* (chicken fat in a pitcher), sours (pickled green tomatoes), utterly delicious cold broiled peppers, and seltzer. The Parkway was born on the lower East Side 50 years ago and recently moved to the heart of the theater district. The only real change, perhaps, is that they now charge 50 cents for the seltzer that once was free on every table. Decor is simple with neat well-spaced tables and blow-ups of fascinating photos depicting the East Side at the turn of the century. Waitresses are helpful: They show you how to mix your mashed potatoes with *greeven* (chicken cracklings) and *schmaltz,* and they may hum what the piped-in radio plays as they serve your dense mushroom and barley soup. They will also tell you, correctly, that the eggplant purée with minced raw onion is terrific. Besides Roumanian broilings you can order stuffed cabbage, *mushk* steak (eye of the rib), and *karnatzlach,* a sausage that definitely is, as the menu proclaims, "for garlic lovers only." There is wine that will never replace the seltzer and there are cocktails—but try slivovitz instead. Everything is à la carte, so lunch can easily mount to $10 and dinner can range from $7 to $15.

THE PARKWAY, 345 West 46th Street, Manhattan. Telephone: (212) 582-7271, 765-0578. Hours: 11:30-4, 4:30-11:30, Monday-Saturday; 3-11:30, Sunday. Cards: AE, BA/Visa, DC, MC. Reservations recommended for dinner. Parking in nearby lot. Full bar service.

Broilings

Karnatzlach (For Garlic Lovers Only) ... 6.50

Roumanian Tenderloin 8.95

Roumanian Tenderloin (For Two) 12.50

Veal Cutlet (Breaded or Broiled) 9.50

Double Baby Lamb Chops 9.95

Calf Sweetbreads 7.95

Sauteed Sweetbreads Over Kasha Varnishkas 7.95

Shell Steak (weight before broiling 1½ lbs) 10.75

Rib Steak 9.50

Mushk Steak 9.50

Broiled Half Spring Chicken 5.95

Broiled Chicken Livers & Unborn Eggs (when available) 6.25

Calf's Liver with Fried Onions 6.95

Chopped Roumanian Tenderloin 5.50

Mixed Grill (4 Person Minimum) 8.50
Consists of Roumanian Tenderloin, Duck, Sweetbreads, Karnatzlach, Chicken Livers and Unborn Eggs (when available)

All of the above served with
Kasha Varnishkas and fresh vegetables

Manhattan: Midtown East
PENG'S
Chinese $

A great Chinese chef who is also a good guy is called "Uncle," and uncles often travel from kitchen to kitchen (and as a corollary, you may be sure, from bank to bank). One such famed practitioner of the Chinese cuisines is Uncle Peng, a former chef to Chiang Kai-Shek, who has now put down roots in his own establishment. Delicacy is not Peng's signature; instead his kitchen turns out earthy, pungent dishes that make you want to lick your chopsticks. When a dish calls for garlic, Peng gives it to you so you remember it later. Spicy dishes are truly spicy (not always the case elsewhere, despite those red triangles on the menu). A darling among his specials is the rich and fragrant minced squab soup, which comes in its own little bamboo container. Among the great main dishes is one simply called vegetable pie; the chief ingredient is that ubiquitous "chameleon" of the Oriental cuisine, bean curd, here in the form of crunchy fried bean curd skins. Another triumph, and the Stendahl Choice, is "chicken prepared in three styles." In this single dish you find three totally different styles of the bird, from bland to peppery, each superb. Honeyed Hunan ham, sautéed lobster balls with hot, spiced ginger sauce, and lamb, either with scallions or in the hot Hunan style, are only a few among many interesting and well-prepared dishes here. Luncheons will average $5.25; dinners about $10 per person.

PENG'S, 219 East 44th Street, Manhattan. Telephone: (212) 682-8050. Hours: 11:30-11, daily. Cards: AE, CB, DC. Reservations suggested. Free parking after 5 pm. Full bar service.

Peng's Specialties

GENERAL TSO'S CHICKEN	5.95
HONEYED HUNAN HAN	6.95
BROILED KING PRAWNS WITH SHELL	7.50
PENG'S SQUID WITH HOT PEPPER SAUCE	7.50
VEGETABLE PIE	7.95
SWEET AND SOUR CRISPY FISH	7.95
LAMB PREPARED IN 2 STYLES	8.95
SAUTEED LOBSTER BALLS WITH HOT SPICED GINGER SAUCE	10.50
SAUTEED SLICED CONCH WITH GARLIC SAUCE	8.75
CHICKEN PREPARED IN 3 STYLES	9.25
FRIED TUNG-PAO CHICKEN	12.00
DRAGON AND PHOENIX	12.00
PEKING DUCK	19.00
SAUTEED SLICED VENISON (Seasonal)	8.50
SAUTEED SLICED PHEASANT (Seasonal)	8.50

Manhattan: Midtown East
PUERTA REAL
Spanish $$

What I like about Puerta Real is that it is precisely non-royal. It is intimate, personal, with good peasanty food and a staff that inclines more to gentle eagerness than cool efficiency. The small menu apparently never changes and features casseroles of chicken, pork or seafood. Plates arrive piled high with food, looking like color photographs in a magazine. Each casserole comes circled by a bed of rice of excellent taste and quality, redolent of wine and meat juices. Salads are tangy and light, and desserts, while few, are on the lush side. *Pinchitos del jefe Antonio,* skewered veal and pork tidbits, is an intriguing appetizer and soups are sturdy. *Pollo en cazeula del jefe* is a soul-satisfying casserole of tender chicken with onions, bacon, potatoes, mushrooms in a wine sauce. *Pollo y langosta al estilo Catalan* combines chicken with lobster in a special seafood sauce. Of course paellas are featured. A typical Spanish treatment of fish is *merluza a la Bilbaina,* in which a juicy filet of marinated hake is striped with sweet red pimientos. Desserts include the inevitable Spanish caramel custard, plus an original concept, *naranjas al caramelo,* caramelized oranges. But only the huskier matadors among us will feel the need for a sweet after the large casseroles. Finally, towards women alone the staff seems as courteous as Spanish knights ever were. Lunches are about $6; dinners $12.50.

PUERTA REAL, 243 East 58th Street, Manhattan. Telephone: (212) 758-4756. Hours: 12-3, 5-11:30, Monday-Saturday; 3-10, Sunday. Cards: AE, BA/Visa, DC, MC. Reservations suggested. Parking in nearby lot. Full bar service.

LANGOSTINOS Y LENGUADO PUERTA REAL $7.50
Spanish Prawns and Grey Sole

ZARZUELA DE MARISCOS DEL JEFE ANTONIO 8.75
Chef's Seafood Casserole Cooked to Perfection

POLLO EN CAZUELA DEL JEFE 6.00
Chicken in Casserole with Small Onions, Bacon, Potatoes, Mushrooms in Wine Sauce

GRAN VILLAGODIO A LAS BRASAS (para dos) 19.00
Broiled Rib of Prime Beef in Red Wine and Shallots Sauce (for two)

ALMEJAS DEL PESCADOR 7.25
Clams in White Wine and Tomato Sauce

MERLUZA A LA KOSKERA 6.50
A Seafood Delight from the Basque Country

LANGOSTA GRATINADA PUERTA REAL 10.00
Lobster Saute in Wine with Lobster Butter and Gratine in Cheese

MERLUZA A LA BILBAINA 6.50
Juicy Filet of Hake Marinated with Sweet Red Pepper Stripes

Manhattan: Midtown East
THE REIDYS'
Irish-American Pub $

The Reidys' leads a charmed life. All around it buildings have been torn down or made into parking lots, but this pleasant Irish-American pub remains steadfast and refuses to give in to runaway inflation. Food is good and man-sized rather than delicate. The dry martinis have purity and power, as if they were still being made for Robert Benchley. The bar bears scars, the bartenders are grizzled but serious, the decor is serviceable and simple. Service is friendly. While The Reidys' is as masculine as a prime sirloin, there is plenty of warm welcome for women, particularly those with hearty appetites. On the flimsy little à la carte menu there are 11 substantial entrées under $5, and the most expensive items are "The Steak" ($7.50), a decent prime sirloin with sautéed onions, and "The New York Filet Mignon" (sic), a good boneless steak with bacon strips. They also have a "Great Big Steak for $8.50, really too big, but you know best." Everything is extra, but even if you order a stingingly dry martini for $1.35, a crock of onion soup for 95 cents and a "black on black" sundae for 75 cents a hearty meal will total up to about $8.50. Who's to complain? Not Stendahl.

THE REIDYS', 22 East 54th Street, Manhattan. Telephone: (212) PL3-2419. Hours: 11:30-1 am, Monday-Saturday; closed Sunday. No credit cards. Reservations suggested. Street parking. Full bar service.

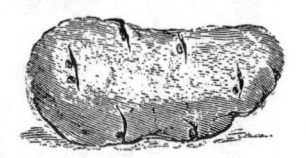

Manhattan: Midtown West
RIO DE JANEIRO
Brazilian/Portuguese

$

There are quite a few Brazilian-Portuguese restaurants around town, many of them invisibly tucked away on a second floor. Rio is more opulent, has more charm and professional service than the others, and is really not much more expensive. There are two drawbacks to Rio. One is the bar area up front, furnished in a seasick-green vinyl, where soiled glasses pile up in an unappetizing way. The second is that the maître d' often wastes time unnecessarily clearing tables or pounding away on the cash register. Once past these annoyances, dining can be fun. Little "on the house" appetizers are popped onto the table even before you order. They include garlicky chorizo sausage and sometimes deliciously spiced baby shrimp. Codfish, of course, is the mainstay of Portugal, and here you can have it, fresh or salted, in a dozen ways. Here, as in Brazil, they feature on Saturday that incredible feast called *feijoada*. In English this means "bean stew," but to me it translates "including the kitchen sink." This monument to gluttony is only $5.50 at Rio and includes mounds of good black beans, mounds of rice and a juicy wine-dark stew made from several different meats. If you insist on being traditional, as you dig in you'll knock back a shot of *cachaca*, the high-powered, down-home Brazilian rum that reminds me of a fiery tequila. The wine list naturally features Portuguese wines, quite nice and modestly priced. Lunches average about $6, dinners $10.

RIO DE JANEIRO, 41 West 57th Street, Manhattan. Telephone: (212) 935-1232. Hours: 12-10, Sunday-Thursday; until 11, Friday-Saturday. Cards: AE, BA/Visa, MC. Reservations not necessary except for large parties. Parking in nearby garage. Full bar service.

Manhattan: Midtown West
ROMEO SALTA
Northern Italian
$$$

Merry and beautiful, diminutive Rosita Salta hops like popcorn from table to table, making sure the food and service match the splendor of the setting. Entering past the iron grillwork of what was once a magnificent town house, you enter a very large area divided into two dining sections. On every wall hang original paintings, mainly of luscious ladies in happy undress. My favorite spot is at the inner banquettes, where I can look across the room through a great glass wall and watch the kitchen team at work. Romeo Salta himself was recalled to duty not far back, after the restaurant slipped momentarily while under a different management, but he is to be seen only at lunchtime now. All the great northern Italian dishes are on the lengthy menu, and quite a few originals. I recommend *gnocchi ai tre sapori,* fluffy miniature dumplings in a dressing compounded of bolognese sauce, fresh tomatoes and whipped cream. Most of the classic pastas are $8.75, enough to serve two. Fish and meats are priced from $11.75 to $13.75 and are all served elegantly. Besides the traditionals, the choice includes such adventurous dishes as *frittura scelta,* an assortment of fried fish that changes seasonally. In winter they feature *bollito misto,* the great Italian boiled dinner, and in summer *vitello tonnato,* the beautiful dish of cold veal in tuna sauce. Not to be missed in any season is *lombatine de vitello al cartoccio,* veal chops with prosciutto and mushrooms, smothered in a wine sauce and sealed in a paper bag until the meat can almost be eaten with a spoon. *Magnifico!* There are no bargains on the wine list, but the selection is a sensitive one.

ROMEO SALTA, 30 West 56th Street, Manhattan. Telephone: (212) 246-5772. Hours: 12-11:30, Monday-Saturday; closed Sunday. Cards: AE, CB, DC, MC. Reservations required. Parking in nearby garage. Full bar service.

Piatti del giorno/Entrees

Scaloppine "ZINGARELLA"—Veal Peppers, Tomatoes, Oregano $11.75

VEAL PAILLARD "ED SULLIVAN" $11.75

Scaloppine "FLORIO"—Veal, Marsala, Wine Mushrooms $11.75

PICCATA di Vitello—Filet of Veal Saute Crispy, Butter, and lemon $11.75

Scaloppine "CHIC MARTINI"—Veal, Butter, Lemon. Parmesan Cheese $11.75

Saltimbocca alla Romana—Veal, Sage. Wine, Prosciutto $11.75

Bollito Misto—Assorted Boiled Dinner, Wintertime only $11.75

Cotoletta di Vitello allà Milanese—Breaded Veal Cutlet $11.75   Ossobuco alla Milanese—Veal Knuckle with Rice $12.75

Cotoletta di Vitello Pizzaiola $11.75   Rognoncino Trifolato—Calf's Kidneys. Wine. Mushrooms $10.75

Cervella alla Napoletana—Calf's Brains, Eggs, Lemon Sauce $11.75

Animelle "GASTRONOMICA"—Calf's Sweetbreads "Argo Dolce" Sauce $11.75

Petto di Pollo "MIMOSA"—Boneless Breast of Chicken, Mozzarella, Prosciutto $11.25

Spezzato di Pollo ROMEO—Chicken in small pieces, white wine & chives $11.25   Veal Valdostana $11.75

Fegato alla Veneziana—Sliced Liver with Onions and White Wine $11.25

Cotoletta alla Bolognese—Veal Cutlet, Mozzarella. Prosciutto $11.75

Cotoletta COLOMBO—Stuffed Veal Chop with Prosciutto and Cheese $11.75   Cotoletta "UGO DRAGO" $11.75

Lombatine di Vitello al cartoccio -- Veal chops with prosciutto and mushrooms, wine sauce in the paper $12.50

Scaloppine Veal GIANNINO $11.75

SCARPARIELLO   Chicken in small pieces and fresh Chicken livers sauteed in olive oil. parsley & a little garlic $10.75

Manhattan: Midtown West
ROSOFF'S
Jewish/American $

When Longacre Square became Times Square in 1903, Rosoff's was already a fixture in the area. At this popular, noisy place, the food is never great, but never bad, either. Yet it remains a New York must because, besides being handy to all theaters, it has many admirable features. Parking for both dinner *and* theater is only $1.50—which alone would make dining at Rosoff's worthwhile. They also provide a special menu for children under 12, a menu in Braille and a very popular non-smoking section. If you're theater-bound, ask your waiter for a "special attention" flag and, if necessary, he will throw you out of the restaurant in time for your curtain. It is no wonder Rosoff's has flourished through the years. The colorful menu of course lists Jewish items such as gefilte fish, chopped chicken livers and matzo ball consommé. But the mainstays are American standbys of chicken, steak and fish. (If you are weight watching, Rosoff's promises to prepare your seafood with lemon or tomato juice or even water, instead of butter.) There are also some Rosoff special combinations: cock 'n' bull (broiled chicken and chopped steak with onion rings) or Laurel and Hardy (broiled jumbo shrimp in garlic butter, plus a tiny filet mignon, topped with onion rings). The magic of Rosoff's permits you to add $2 to any main dish and come up with a complete dinner. If you dine at Rosoff's, you will never leave hungry. Lunch is about $5; dinner from $8.50.

ROSOFF'S, 147 West 43rd Street, Manhattan. Telephone: (212) 582-3200. Hours: 11:30-9, Sunday-Thursday; until midnight, Friday-Saturday. Cards: AE, BA/Visa, CB, DC, MC. Reservations suggested. Discount for dinner and theater parking after 5:30 pm. Full bar service.

BROILED PRIME CHOPPED SIRLOIN STEAK Nothing added but the touch of flame. We crown it with crisp onion rings. ... 5.95

BROILED HALF FRESH SPRING CHICKEN A carefully chosen plump and meaty bird. Butter basted and cooked to a turn. ... 5.95

ROAST BREAST OF TURKEY A LA MAISON Chef's gravy and cranberry compote. ... 6.95

BROILED BUTCHER'S TENDERLOIN STEAK A juicy cut, especially delicious when ordered rare. Crowned with crisp French fried onion rings. ... 8.95

BROILED FRESH FILLET OF LEMON SOLE AU BEURRE This is the best fish dish in New York City. ... 7.95

FRESH NEW BEDFORD SCALLOPS As you prefer, broiled in butter, or fried golden brown. ... 7.95

FRIED BUTTERFLY JUMBO SHRIMP ... 9.95

SHRIMP SCAMPI A LA GEORGE Juicy Shrimp, broiled in butter with a touch of garlic. ... 9.95

Manhattan: Midtown West
THE RUSSIAN TEA ROOM
Russian $$

The Russian Tea Room is unique in many ways, not the least being that its waiters are perhaps the rudest in town. I've seen patrons in yelling arguments with them. I've sat at a long table where our waiter passed our soups down in a forced fire-bucket brigade. And it seems to me I've narrowly escaped being challenged to a saber duel with flaming shish kebab skewers. For 50 years, however, TRT has been serving authentic Russian food to a host of tourists, Russians, musicians, artists and celebrities, and it is still frequently necessary to stand in line for a table. Waiting is almost fun because of the multilingual, multigenerational crowd that packs the place. A seat at the bar is fascinating: You are apt to overhear your neighbors planning a liaison, making a swap of an armchair for a cello, or analyzing the influence of the Beatles on symphonic music. There are excellent vodkas from everywhere, and five kinds of caviar on the menu. The borscht, served hot with sour cream and *pirojok* (tiny meat pastries), is fabulous; *karsky shaslik suprême* (a Cossack-sized serving of superbly barbecued lamb cutlet) is unbeatable; and the chicken Kiev is guaranteed to spurt butter when pierced. Every day a special dish is featured. My favorite is the Wednesday special, *pelmeny* Siberian, which is chopped beef and veal dumplings served in a dill-spiked consommé, with mustard sauce and sour cream. Wines are modestly priced, and tea comes in the traditional glass instead of a cup. *Table d'hôte* dinners range from $9 to $15.75.

THE RUSSIAN TEA ROOM, 150 West 57th Street, Manhattan. Telephone: (212) 265-0947. Hours: 11:30 am-1 am, daily; until 2 am, Saturday. Cards: AE, BA/Visa, CB, DC, MC. Reservations suggested. Parking in nearby garage. Full bar service.

Appetizers

RTR Zakuska
(Hors d'Oeuvres a La Russe, 1.50 extra)
Kholodetz
Pickled Herring in Sour Cream
Swedish Matjes Herring
Eggplant Orientale
Mushrooms a La Grecque
Chopped Chicken Livers
Grapefruit or Melon (in season)
Choice of Juices

Soups with Pirojok

Hot Borscht with Sour Cream
Cold Borscht with Sour Cream (in Season)
Green Schi (Cream of Spinach)
Consomme with Egg Noodles

Entrees

RTR Specialty of the Day
Eggplant a La Russe, au Gratin—10.25
Karsky Shashlik Supreme—15.75
Cotelette a La Kiev—14.00   Cotelette de Volaille—14.25
Mushrooms a La Russe, au Gratin—10.25
Shashlik Caucasian—14.50
Blinchiki with Cheese and Sour Cream—9.75
Sirniki with Sour Cream—9.00   Nalistniki—9.75
Luli Kebab—9.75   Beef a La Stroganoff—13.25
Kulebiaka—10.25
Cotelettes Boyar—9.75
Pilaff of Spring Lamb—10.00
Beef Duchesse, Mushroom Sauce—10.25
Broiled Striped Sea Bass, Lemon Butter Sauce—10.25

Manhattan: Midtown West
SARDI'S
Continental

$$

Sardi's theatrical star still shines through the tarnish of time. As lushly described on its menu, Sardi's is "post office, message center, lovers' rendezvous, eating trough, drinking hole ... and a psychiatrist's couch for the professional theater." Not a bad portrait. The "eating trough" quite often lacks delicacy, but never quantity. I have always liked Sardi's because the casual out-of-towners who come to gawk are treated no more abruptly than a Broadway star. The waiters are not really indifferent, they are just businessmen with a lot on their minds and on their trays. But they will get you to your table and out in time for the theater, and they will seat your Aunt Belle next to a name from stage, screen or tube as if she were a celebrity herself. The Stendahl Choice has eternally been the *cannelloni au gratin,* (not so good as an appetizer, but a very good main course). Two giant crêpes are plump with a magic mixture of chicken hash and spinach with a thick brown sauce, topped with grated cheese. The worst items are the synthetic "Oriental Dishes, Continental Style," a hangover from an era better forgotten. Wines are moderately priced. A hearty lunch may hit $10 and dinners build from about $12 up. The unadorned upstairs that once was packed with unknowns, has reversed itself and is now the "in" place for young theater folk, with their own popular bar.

SARDI'S, 234 West 44th Street, Manhattan. Telephone: (212) 221-8440. Hours: 11:30-1 am, daily. Cards: AE, BA/Visa, DC, MC. Reservations suggested. Parking in nearby garages. Full bar service.

Sardi's LUNCHEON

CHEF'S SUGGESTIONS

Veal Cutlet Viennoise: Anchovies and Capers, Egg Crumbles and Creamed Chopped Spinach	9.95
Scallopine of Veal Piemontaise with Yellow Rice and Peas	9.95
Calf's Liver Emincé, Sauté Veneziana, Whipped Potatoes	6.95
Emincé of Chicken Espagnole, Rice, Peas and Mixed Green Salad	6.95
Fresh Calf's Liver Sauté in Butter, with Bacon, Baked Potato and Mixed Green Salad	9.95
Sliced London Broil, Zucchini, Home Fries	8.95
Chopped Veal Steak, Poached Egg and Peas, Sauce Diable	6.95

ORIENTAL DISHES (CONTINENTAL STYLE)

Chicken Curry 6.95   Lamb Curry 8.95   Shrimp Curry 9.95
Curry Dishes are Served with Rice, Peas, Chutney and Pompadoms
Chicken Chow Mein, Rice and Fried Noodles 6.50
Shrimp Chow Mein, Rice and Fried Noodles 7.95

FROM THE BROILER

Sirloin Steak of Prime Beef 13.95   Minute Sirloin Steak of Prime Beef 11.95
Prime Filet Mignon 13.95   Double Rib Lamb Chops (2) 11.95
Brochette of Beef on Rice Pilaff, Green Peas 8.95
Chopped Sirloin Steak with Baked Potato and Mixed Green Salad 9.95
Broiled Half Chicken with Baked Potato and Mixed Green Salad 7.95
Broiled Fresh Mushrooms on Toast with Mixed Green Salad 5.95
Side Order of Broiled Mushrooms (served only with Main Course) 2.50
Garlic Bread .75 per person

SEAFARE

Fresh Deep Sea Scallops, Cole Slaw and Peas,	Fried 8.75	Broiled 9
Broiled Striped Bass, Brown Button Capers Sauce, Boiled Potato		8
Fresh Filler of Sole, Cole Slaw and Peas	Fried 7.50	Broiled 7
Fried Frogs' Legs, Cole Slaw and Peas		9
King Crab, Shrimp, Deep Sea Scallops à la Newburg, Rice and Peas		10

VEGETABLES

Hot Vegetable Plate with Poached Egg 6.50
Broccoli with Hollandaise or Butter Sauce 2.75
Braised Lettuce with Mushroom and Bacon 1.50
Plain Spinach 1.50   Creamed 1.75   Fresh String Beans 1.50
Fresh Zucchini 1.50   Garden Peas 1.10
Baked Potato 1.25; with Sour Cream and Chives 1.75
French Fried Potatoes 1.10   Boiled Potato 1.10
Creamed Whipped Potatoes 1.10

Manhattan: Midtown West
THE SANCTUARY
American $

Looking for the cheapest *good* meal in New York? How about dining for under $10 in a candlelight setting, at a buffet that offers plenty of salad mixings and vegetables, a choice of several good plain American main dishes, and with an opportunity to return for a second helping? Did I say $10? How about $3.95? Of course, if you insist on a beverage and dessert, they come extra. But you can have them, and all the above-mentioned items, too, for a grand total of—$5.70! (The buffet lunch is only $2.95.) In New York it is really easy to dine well for $10 or less. If you search around. Most such bargains are ethnic hideaways, family-run establishments that often serve more authentic foods than fancier places. But to find decent *American* cuisine in New York is difficult at any price. To find it at a tops of $5.70 for a complete dinner is marvelous. Add on the candlelight and it becomes a minor miracle. A typical buffet might include a choice of four such down-home favorites as meat loaf, hamburger and onions, chicken fricasee, roast turkey, even roast beef. The Sanctuary is located in the landmark site of the old theatrical Lamb's Club, and is operated by the Manhattan Church of the Nazarene. It may disturb some, but I cry "hurrah" at the footnote that the Sanctuary is a "no-smoking environ."

THE SANCTUARY, 130 West 44th Street, Manhattan. Telephone: (212) 575-0300. Hours: 11:30-2:30, 5-8, Monday-Saturday; closed Sunday. No credit cards. Reservations not accepted. Street parking. No alcoholic beverages.

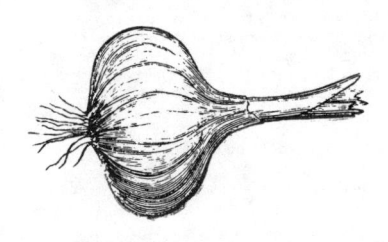

Manhattan: Chinatown
SAY ENG LOOK
Shanghai/Chinese $

One small room, bare formica tables, no decor except for napkins of cloth instead of paper—yet customers stand in line halfway out in the street waiting for a table. On every visit you see new, mysterious and tantalizing bowls and platters arriving at the table next to your elbow. Ordering what my neighbors were eating introduced me to a delight simply titled "sweet and sour yellow whole fish." This giant boned fish, deep fried in a thin batter, is incredibly crisp on the outside, moist within. It arrives swimming in an orange-red sweet and sour sauce and covered with tiny carrot cubes, bamboo shoots, a bit of crunchy onion, baby shrimp and a few peas. A splendid base dish for a dinner for four. Of the unique seasonal specials, a most excellent choice is fried roll fish with bean curd sheet. These look like egg rolls, but are actually flaky white fish bits wrapped in tissue-thin bean curd skin. "Puff with fresh pork chop meat" is a sauce of finely minced pork covering spongy dollops of semi-fried bean curd—highly unusual in texture and taste. Popular also is subgum casserole, a pretty pottery bowl of broth packed with transparent noodles, seafoods, vegetables and meats. Waiters are busy swabbing tables for the next invasion, but when you catch one he is knowledgeable, patient and often witty. Tea is fine—pale and blossomy with a faint natural sweetness. Beer and soft drinks are on hand; if you want other beverages, bring your own. Prices vary with the season, but the most expensive dish I've tried here was only $6.

SAY ENG LOOK, 1 East Broadway, off Chatham Square, Manhattan. Telephone: (212) 732-0796, 233-9598. Hours: 11:30-10:30, Sunday-Thursday; until 11:30, Friday-Saturday. Cards: MC. Reservations not accepted. Street parking. Beer only.

Manhattan: Midtown West
SEA FARE OF THE AÉGEAN
Seafood $$

There are only about five top-level seafood restaurants in New York, alas. Sea Fare of the Aegean is one of them. It is impressive, built on three levels and decorated with original art, some of superior quality. There is a grand staircase, deep coral walls, and plenty of space between tables. Sometimes service seems scanty, calling for a few more captains and waiters. Otherwise, Sea Fare cannot be faulted. As one of the captains said, "If other places get their fish the same way we buy ours—the freshest, best available, then there can't be much difference between their cooking and ours." What is different, however, is that Sea Fare has a list of specialties all its own, in addition to the standards found on every fishy menu. (The menu itself here is a work of art, a veritable book, illustrated in color, five pages long.) Oysters are plump and fresh, shrimp are plump and fresh, fish is deftly cooked and fresh. So? So let us look at some of the Sea Fare's originals. Red snapper soup Aegean is creamy, suave, scented—a must. A highlight among main dishes is plump jumbo shrimps baked en casserole with feta cheese, grilled tomato, and a fabulous Santorini-style sauce—a pi-

SEA FARE SPECIALTIES

IMPORTED DOVER SOLE SAUTEED IN GARLIC SAUCE	13.65
BROILED COMBINATION SEAFOOD PLATTER WITH LOBSTER TAIL	14.75
LOBSTER, CRAB MEAT & SHRIMP A LA NEWBURG, SAUTE or AU GRATIN	14.25
INDIVIDUAL FLOUNDER STUFFED WITH CRAB MEAT	12.25
BOUILLABAISSE MARSEILLAISE	14.75
JUMBO SHRIMPS STUFFED WITH CRAB MEAT	13.25
ALASKAN KING CRAB WITH MELTED BUTTER	13.95
JUMBO SHRIMPS BROILED or SAUTE-MUSTARD SAUCE	12.25
BABY LOBSTER TAILS STUFFED WITH LUMP CRAB MEAT	13.85
SOLE SEAFARE EN CASSEROLE WITH ASPARAGUS AU GRATIN	10.25
BROOK TROUT STUFFED WITH CRAB MEAT	12.45

ALL ABOVE DISHES SERVED WITH GREEN SALAD AND FRENCH FRIED POTATOES

quant, tomatoey creation. The same great dish can be had with baby lobster tails instead of shrimp. Other Aegean casseroles feature creative sauces, and they are based on poached red snapper, filet of lemon sole stuffed with crabmeat, steamed striped bass, and so on. A fish Cretan style is succulent in its own broth, seasoned with delicate green herbs. Andros style means the same delicate fish comes in avgolemono soup—a broth lip-tingling with fresh lemon. There are also seafood salads, Creole dishes and curries. For the non-Neptunian there is only one choice, chicken. While the house is proud of its Greek desserts, I have found the baclava and flogiara rather dry instead of melting in honey syrup. The wine list is a good one, well priced, and features Greek, California and German wines. There is also a choice of 13 beers. *Table d'hôte* luncheons are $8.25 up, and main dishes on the dinner begin at $7.25. Those splendid casseroles are about $13.

SEA FARE OF THE AEGEAN, 25 West 56th Street, Manhattan. Telephone: (212) 581-0540. Hours: 12-11, Monday-Saturday; 1-11, Sunday. Cards: AE, BA/Visa, CB, DC, MC. Reservations suggested. Parking in nearby garages. Full bar service.

AEGEAN SPECIALTIES

STRIPED BASS EN CASSEROLE (AEGEAN STYLE) BAKED WITH WINE SAUCE AND CHERRYSTONE CLAMS	12.25
JUMBO SHRIMPS (SANTORINI STYLE) BAKED EN CASSEROLE WITH FETA CHEESE GRILLED TOMATO AND SANTORINI SAUCE	13.85
POACHED RED SNAPPER WITH WHITE AVGOLEMONO SAUCE (SCORPIOS STYLE) SERVED WITH YOUNG CARROTS AND BOILED POTATO	12.65
BAKED FILET OF LEMON SOLE STUFFED WITH CRAB MEAT (SKOPELOS STYLE), SERVED WITH GRILLED PARMESAN TOMATO AND GREEN PEAS	13.25
STEAMED STRIPED BASS EN CASSEROLE (ANDROS STYLE) SERVED WITH ITS OWN AVGOLEMONO SOUP	12.85
STEAMED FILET OF STRIPED BASS EN CASSEROLE (CRETAN STYLE) SERVED WITH FRESH GREEN HERBS AND ITS OWN BROTH	12.85
STEAMED RED SNAPPER EN CASSEROLE (SYROS STYLE)	13.65
STEAMED STRIPED BASS EN CASSEROLE (RODOS STYLE) WITH MIXED GROUND HERBS AND SHERRY WINE SERVED WITH ITS OWN SOUP	12.85
BABY LOBSTER TAILS (SANTORINI STYLE) BAKED EN CASSEROLE WITH FETA CHEESE GRILLED TOMATO AND SANTORINI SAUCE	14.85

Manhattan: Midtown East
SIAMESE GARDENS
Thai

$

Thai restaurants are popping up like little hot peppers all around us. The first Thais established a tiny kingdom along Eighth Avenue, just above the theater district. One of these restaurants sold its name and reopened as the Siamese Gardens on the far-away East Side. The owners, however, were carried away by their new surroundings only to the extent of housing themselves in a weird little shingled bungalow; their prices remained as low as they ever were. All the Thai restaurants in New York I have sampled have tamed their fiery cuisine for Caucasian tastes. The Gardens goes one step further and offers little boats of hot sauce that you can ladle on as your palate pleads. Luncheon here is a good place to begin exploring Thai cuisine: For $3 to $7 you can sample a long list of specialties, such as fried noodles with pork, bean sauce and broccoli; sweet squid sautéed with onion; or even a combination plate featuring a shrimp fritter, spicy squid sauté and chicken with bamboo shoots. At night they hand you a kingly red or blue velvet book that lists more formal—and exotic—dishes. *Phad Thai* is fried rice noodles with bean sprouts, chives, egg, ground shrimp and peanuts. Delicious. There is an outstanding soup, *tom yum kunk,* plump with "halfmoon shrimps," peppers, mushrooms and lemon grass. The Stendahl Choice here is *plaa thod,* whole baked red snapper, smothered in assorted vegetables, with bits of pork and a tantalizing mild sauce. Dinner entrées are in the $7 range. Another world, and an inexpensive one, is Siamese Gardens.

SIAMESE GARDENS, 220 East 53rd Street, Manhattan. Telephone: (212) 935-1920. Hours: 11:30-11, Monday-Saturday; 5-11, Sunday. Cards: AE, BA/Visa, MC. Reservations suggested on weekends. Parking in nearby garage. Bring your own beer or wine.

Fruit de Mer

Phad Saam Gir = Squid In Love. — $ 5.95
The combination of squid, chicken and shrimp saute with hot pepper and herbs.

Plaa Gean = Fried Red Snapper. — $ 6.95
Wonderfully crisp browned skin fish, simmered in sauce of chilli and various herbs.

Plaa Thod = Regal Red Snapper. — $ 7.25
Bake whole fish, smother with assorted vegetables, pork and sauce.

Plaa Nyp = Steamed Fish. — $ 7.25
Authentically fragrant fish with pork, mushroom, ginger and aromatic of coriander.

Kunn Piaw Wann = Sweet & Sour Jumbo Shrimps. — $ 6.95

Kunn Phad Yod Khawphool = Shrimps saute with baby corns. — $ 6.95

Kunn Phow = Broiled Shrimps. — $ 6.95

Manhattan: Lower East Side
SWEETS
Seafood $$

Down by the docks of the old Fulton Fish Market, now site of the fascinating museum of old ships, South Side Seaport, is Sweets, a romantic remnant of early New York. The salty old restaurant has recently celebrated its 135th year, with only the Sweets and Lake families managing in all that time. I knew all about Sweets before I ever thought to come to New York, and it seems to have changed little, if memory holds. On occasion there is still that lineup on the steep stairs, patiently waiting their turn to get inside and sit at the worn tables. A chin-whisker attitude survives in a line still carried on the menu: "The Management will Appreciate your reporting any Discourtesy on the part of the Employees. Thank you." As to the menu, non-seafood lovers go home. Aside from a few omelettes, some vegetables, desserts and dill pickles, Sweets serves seafood exclusively. You may be assured it is some of the freshest available, now as always. Everything is à la carte, so a few prices might guide you. Chowder is $1.50 a "plate"; $1.25 a cup. Oysters broiled in butter, $5.95. Lobster salad, $9.50. Broiled fish ranges from $3.95 for mackerel to $9.95 for Eastern halibut. Lobster and crabmeat Newburg is $9.95, lobster and crabmeat salad, $9.50. One would expect a nice list of white wines in an all-finny restaurant. Not so, but there are eight good beers and ales for comfort. Don't argue with Sweets.

SWEETS, 2 Fulton Street, Manhattan. Telephone: (212) 825-9786, 344-9189. Hours: 11:30-8:30, Monday-Friday; closed Saturday-Sunday. No credit cards. Reservations not accepted. Street parking. Full bar service.

Sea Food (to order)

BROILED SHAD	9.95
BROILED SHAD ROE (2) with Bacon	12.25
BROILED FINNAN HADDIE	6.95
FINNAN HADDIE A LA SWEETS	7.50
FINNAN HADDIE AU GRATIN	7.95
BROILED SWORDFISH	9.95
BROILED OR FRIED L. I. BAY SCALLOPS	8.95
BROILED RED SNAPPER	9.25
BROILED SEA BASS	6.95
BROILED SCROD COD	4.95
BROILED EASTERN HALIBUT	9.95
BROILED STRIPED BASS	7.95
BROILED MACKEREL	3.50
BROILED BLUEFISH	5.50
BROILED FILET OF HADDOCK, Tartar Sauce	7.95
FILET OF GREY SOLE, Tartar Sauce	9.95
CRABMEAT A LA NEWBURG	9.25
LOBSTER AND CRABMEAT NEWBURG	9.95
CRABMEAT SAUTE 9.25 CRABMEAT AU GRATIN	9.50
CODFISH STEAK	5.75
COMBINATION SEAFOOD NEWBURG	9.95
SHRIMP CREOLE with Rice	9.25
SHRIMPS NEWBURG ... 9.25 SHRIMPS AU GRATIN	9.50
FRIED SHRIMPS 8.95 SHRIMPS SAUTE	9.25
LOBSTER AU GRATIN 9.95 LOBSTER NEWBURG	9.95

(Above Entrees served with Potato du Jour or Rice)

Manhattan: Midtown West
SWISS CENTER RESTAURANTS
FONDUE POT and PAVILION
Swiss $$

The Swiss enjoy four culinary accents: German, French, Italian and Romanche (a tiny minority of mountain folk with their own language and customs). Often the same classics are served by different names, notably the famous veal creation the German-Swiss call *Zurcher geschnetzeltes* and the French-Swiss call *emince de veau Zurichoise.* Thus the menus of the two Swiss Center restaurants are multilingual. In a bright chalet-like ambience downstairs, the Fondue Pot serves a limited menu of delicious specialties, while upstairs the more formal Pavilion charges more and serves a wider range of dishes. The Zurich veal delicacy, for example, lists at $8.50 down in the farmyard and $9.50 in classical surroundings upstairs, but the same kitchen provides both plates. This is a memorable dish: Tender medallions of finest white veal swim in a luscious cream-wine sauce, speckled with mushrooms. On the side is a serving of *rösti*, traditional Swiss potato shreds fried into a crunchy pancake. Somewhat similar but even richer and available only at Pavilion is *vols-au-vent "Marcel,"* two puff pastry

Pavilion

Zürcher Geschnetzeltes
9.50
Next to fondue, the most popular Swiss specialty: sliced veal and mushrooms in cream sauce. Rösti potatoes

Kalbsleber Thurgauer-Art
10.50
Sliced calf's liver and apples, sauteed. Fried onions and parsley potatoes

Rahmschnitzel
12.00
Veal cutlets with cream sauce. Sauteed champignons and imported Swiss noodles

shells filled with creamed veal and mushrooms, this time adorned with a broiled tomato shell filled with fresh peas. *Rahmschnitzel* (also in the Pavilion) is almost the same, but more expensive because of superb noodles imported from Switzerland at more than $3 per pound! Less caloric but tasty are items such as delicious bratwurst, a Swiss sauerbraten, and a delicate trout sautéed with grapes. Fondues and the famous specialty, *raclette,* are also available. Exclusively at Pavilion are flambées, among which is a unique *huhnerbrustchen mit orangen,* chicken breast stuffed with veal, nuts and honey, flamed in Curaçao. Notable is the wine list—more than 30 wines from everywhere in Switzerland, 15 of which are unobtainable anywhere else in this country. Whites generally go best with the suave foods.

FONDUE POT and PAVILION, Swiss Center, 4 West 49th Street, Manhattan. Telephone: (212) 247-6545. Fondue Pot hours: 12:30-3:30, Monday-Friday; until 6:30, Saturday; closed Sunday. Pavilion hours: 12-2:30, Monday; 12-2:30, 5-10, Tuesday-Friday; 5-11, Saturday; closed Sunday. Cards: AE, BA/Visa, CB, DC, MC. Reservations suggested in the evening. Validated parking in nearby garage from 5:30-1 am, Monday-Friday; noon-1 am, Saturday. Full bar service.

Vols-au-Vent "Marcel"
8.50
Puff pastry shells filled with veal and mushrooms in a light cream sauce. Served with broiled tomato filled with green peas

Piccata con Limone
9.00
Veal cutlets sauteed in a light wine sauce with a touch of lemon. Broiled tomato and choice of imported Swiss noodles or rice

Pavilion

Foie de Veau Emincé
9.00
Minced calf's liver in a light red wine sauce with Rosti potatoes or rice

Manhattan: Upper West Side
SZECHUAN RESTAURANT
Chinese (Szechwan)

$

Some of the best Chinese restaurants in Manhattan are not in Chinatown, but along upper Broadway. The entrance to this little restaurant is so modest that many pass it by with never a thought of entering. The decor inside matches the humble exterior—a long narrow box of a room, with well-spaced tables and simple booths along both sides. Yet it may well be here that the Szechwan cuisine was introduced to New Yorkers eight years ago. (At least it was the first place with an exclusively Szechwan menu; I enjoyed a few of these peppery dishes in the venerable Shanghai on Broadway as early as the fifties.) Service is by men and young women in casual dress who, while not garrulous, respond helpfully in translating some of the terms on the menu. Throughout the years, the quality of Szechuan's kitchen has remained first-rate. Dishes are authentically and carefully made; none ever disappoints. When you see "home-style" after an item, that means it is truly spicy. Noodles with bean sauce is an excellent version of this classic, and it comes Peking style (mild) and Szechwan style (piquant). Highlights include shredded beef, dry-sautéed Szechwan style, and carp in hot bean sauce with ham and pork shreds. A personal favorite is the mildly seasoned Szechwan dumpling with soup, or a much zestier version with red hot oil. This is a lip-tingling broth, in either case, heaped high with meat-filled dumplings with deliciously slippery won ton skins. Two persons can dine heartily here for $10.

SZECHUAN, 2536 Broadway, Manhattan. Telephone: (212) 663-8150. Hours: 12-11, Sunday-Thursday; until midnight, Friday-Saturday. Cards: AE, BA/Visa. Reservations suggested on weekends. Street parking. No bar service; bring your own liquor.

SHRIMP AND LOBSTER

Sauteed Shrimp with Green Peas	3.75
Sauteed Shrimp with Tomato Sauce	3.85
Plain Sauteed Shrimp	3.95
Sauteed Shrimp with Hot Pepper Sauce	3.95
Sauteed Shrimp with Chili Sauce	3.95
Sweet and Sour Prawns	4.25
Sliced Prawns with Garlic Sauce	4.25
Prawns with Chili Sauce	4.25
Sauteed Lobster, Szechuan Style	6.25

FISH

Plain Sauteed Scallops	3.95
Scallops with Hot Garlic Sauce	3.95
Scallops with Hot Pepper Sauce	3.95
Carp with Bean Curd	3.95
Carp with Brown Sauce	5.25
Carp with Hot Bean Sauce	5.25
Sweet and Sour Fish	5.25

BEEF

Shredded Beef with Green Pepper	3.55
Beef with Bean Curd	3.55
Shredded Beef with Bean Sauce	3.55
Beef with Mushrooms and Bamboo Shoots	3.80
Shredded Beef, Home Style	3.80
Sliced Beef with Scallions	3.80
Shredded Beef with Peking Sauce	3.95
Shredded Beef with Hot Pepper Sauce	3.95
Shredded Beef with Garlic Sauce	3.95
Shredded Beef Dry-Sauteed, Szechuan Style	3.95

PORK

Shredded Pork with Green Pepper	3.35
Moo-Shu Pork (20¢ each thin pancake)	3.35
Shredded Pork with Szechuan Pickled Cabbage	3.35
Sliced Pork with Scallions	3.55
Double Sauteed Sliced Pork	3.55
Sliced Pork with Bean Sauce	3.55
Sauteed Sliced Pork	3.55
Sweet and Sour Pork	3.55
Shredded Pork with Peking Sauce	3.75
Sliced Pork Home Style	3.75
Sliced Pork with Garlic Sauce	3.75

Manhattan: Midtown East
TANDOOR
Indian $

This is another of the regal Indian restaurants and one of my favorites. Decor is palatial: gleaming carved woods, walls bright with fascinating cloth hangings and mellow light from an array of filigree metal globes. A sari-clad maiden, her hands in prayerful attitude, welcomes you; a bewhiskered gentleman in a tight turban escorts you to your table. The red plush banquettes are romantic, but I prefer a table near the big window behind which experts juggle meats and breads as they do their tandoori cooking. Lunch here is a bargain: Upstairs in the back is a room in barren contrast to the elegance below. But here you may scrutinize a dozen or so steaming trays of Indian delicacies, sampling as much as you want from each for only $4.95. The dinner menu also features a bargain, the Special Tandoori Dinner. For $8.95 you receive generous samples of tandoori-broiled chicken, lamb kebab, sausage kebab, chicken *tikka*, a curried meat and a curried vegetable, rounded off with a bit of pilaf, some *dal* (lentil purée) and a *nan*, the light leavened bread that is slapped right onto the side of the blistering tandoor and baked in minutes. The Stendahl Choice is lamb *pasanda*, a marvelous dish of non-gristly, fat-free lamb, served in a suave sauce of nuts and spices mingled with thick cream. Husky Indian beer is available.

TANDOOR, 40 East 49th Street, Manhattan. Telephone: (212) 752-3334. Hours: 11:30-2:30, 5:30-11, Monday-Saturday; 5:30-11, Sunday. Cards: AE, BA/Visa, CB, DC, MC. Reservations suggested. Parking in nearby garage. Full bar service.

> **Special Tandoori Dinner**
> **8.95**
> Tandoori Chicken, Boti Kebab,
> Sheekh Kebab, Chicken Tikka
> Rogan Josh or Beef Kurma &
> Vegetable Curry, Pillaf, Dal, Nan,
> chutney pickles

TANDOOR SPECIALTIES

Tandoori Chicken (Full) (Half)   **6.75** **4.75**
Chicken marinated in yogurt and mild spices with its natural juices, roasted in our clay oven

Reshmi Kebab   **5.75**
Cubes of tender chicken marinated and roasted to a perfect turn in our clay oven

Kalmi Kebab   **4.75**
Chicken legs marinated and roasted in a charcoal clay oven

Chicken Tikka   **4.75**
Thick & juicy cubes of chicken roasted in a clay oven

Boti Kabab   **5.75**
Cubed leg of lamb, broiled to perfection on skewers

Sheekh Kebab   **4.75**
Chopped meat mixed with onions & herbs, roasted on skewers

Tandoori Fish Tikka   **5.75**
Fish pieces delicately marinated & broiled Tandoor style

Tandoori Shrimps   **8.75**
Shrimps roasted Tandoori style

Tandoor Mixed Grill   **7.75**
Assortment of Tandoor Specialties

Manhattan: Midtown East
TORREMOLINOS
Spanish $$

Most Spanish restaurants around New York are modest places that serve hearty food at family prices. Torremolinos serves less hearty food at higher prices, and in a comparatively sophisticated setting. Entering evokes a summery Mediterranean memory: a darkish bar with high stools, a wine-rack wall, beyond an archway a whitewashed patio-like room. Crisp white cloths gleam on tables, spaced well apart. Friendly waiters in black jackets and white shirts skim about like slim toreros. The à la carte menu lists all the Spanish specialties, but they are prepared much more delicately than at most similar restaurants. *Crema de alubias* is a near-perfect black bean soup, hearty, yet suave. *Gazpacho,* on the other spoon, is sometimes a bit too understated. *Zarzuela de mariscos Mediterraneo* is a shellfish and seafood casserole, a Spanish version of the French bouillabaisse. *Paella Valenciana* comes with plenty of juicy morsels of chicken, seafood and bits of chorizo sausage, imbedded in a mountain of moist, tangy rice. One of the best of its kind. *Pollo al ajillo* is a dish of tender chicken sautéed with lemon and a good zip of garlic. The wine list presents, at very decent prices, some splendid Spanish Rioja wines. Better than any of the desserts is a spectacularly good *café Torremolinos,* rich coffee topped with Spanish brandy and then flamed. *Fantastico!* Dinners will average about $16; lunches a few dollars less.

TORREMOLINOS, 230 East 51st Street, Manhattan. Telephone: (212) 755-1862. Lunch: 12-3, Monday-Friday. Dinner: 5:30-11, Monday-Thursday; until midnight, Friday-Saturday; closed Sunday. Cards: AE, CB, DC, MC. Reservations suggested. Street parking. Full bar service.

Especialidades

POLLO CON LANGOSTA CADAQUES 10.50
Chicken & Lobster in Casserole

ZARZUELA DE MARISCOS MEDITERRANEO 10.50
Casserole of Shell Fish & Sea Food

CHULETON DE TERNERA AL JEFE 9.75
Veal Chops Chef's Specialty

VILLAGODIO A LAS BRASAS (PARA DOS) ... 23.00
Double Prime Rib of Beef (for two)

CARRE DE CORDERO LECHAL (PARA DOS) . 24.50
Rack of Baby Lamb (for two)

PAELLA VALENCIANA (FOR TWO) 19.00

PAELLA VALENCIANA WITH LOBSTER . 21.00
(FOR TWO)

Specialties

Manhattan: Midtown West
"21" CLUB
International $$$

The quotation marks in the name of this world-famous restaurant should be around "club" instead of 21. For it is a public eating place, no matter how many old-time patrons insist that it is a fortress that discourages assault by mere citizens and other tourists. While I have always gone incognito, I have never been snubbed or elbowed (except perhaps by customers). Sometimes I have not been seated on the ground floor near the bar, but upstairs, "beyond the pale," for which I have been grateful. In the pubby downstairs, where toy airplanes and cars hang in schoolboy fetish from the ceiling, the regulars sit and call for telephones to be plugged in at their tables. Upstairs supposedly is reserved for "foreigners," but there my elbow has rubbed those of a senator and our current mayor. I outrageously suggest that the service is more elegant upstairs for everyone. "21" is possibly the most famous New York restaurant, certainly

ENTREES
    Royal Squab Grillé, Champignon 14 00
      Escalopine of Veal, Charleroi 14 25
        Baron of Lamb Rôti, Judic 14 25
          Sweetbreads Sauté, Princesse 13 00
            Half Long Island Duckling, Montmorency 13 **50**
              Roast Sirloin of Beef, Boulangère 16 00

one of the most expensive, and there is an annoying $1.50 cover charge. Long arguments have ensued debating whether this unique relic deserves its reputation. So listen. I have never been awed by any of the food served here, but I have enjoyed many meals by staying with the simpler dishes and savoring splendid bottles of wine from an impressive cellar. There are good buys in almost any price range, sommeliers who are eager to steer you in the right direction, and a staggering page or two of treasures. Greatest adventure of all here is a trip down below ground, where a great wall of rock swings open to reveal a secret treasure house of liquors, from way before prohibition, as well as champagnes stashed away for presidents. Visits are not always possible, but if you consult your waiter at the beginning of your meal, a little gnome may lead you to the mysteries.

"21" CLUB, 21 West 52nd Street, Manhattan. Telephone: (212) 582-7221. Hours: 12-12, daily. Cards: AE, BA/Visa, CB, DC, MC. Reservations suggested. Parking in nearby garage. Full bar service.

POISSONS

English Sole Poché, Duglére 14 50
Long Island Bay Scallops, Fines Herbes 13 50
Swordfish Steak Grillé, Stanley 13 25
Red Snapper Grillé, Choron 12 00
Brook Trout Sauté, Amandine 13 00
Frogs' Legs Sauté, Provençale 13 00

Manhattan: Midtown East
UNCLE TAI'S HUNAN YUAN
Chinese (Hunan)

$$

While the food here is reasonably authentic, the ambience at Uncle Tai's suggests to me Victorian England. Appointments are gently understated and service is quietly sophisticated. The food looks neat upon the plate, but it is also geared too nicely to the American palate. What makes Uncle Tai's garden worth a visit is the array of fascinating dishes (whether absolutely authentic or not) that are not available at other Chinese restaurants in New York. Honeyed ham with dates is one intriguing appetizer. Another is diced boneless squab that you wrap in lettuce leaves, a sort of Chinese taco. Few Chinese places offer cold peppered rabbit or crispy slices of pig ear in hot, spicy oil (the pig ear, to the uninitiated, is unidentifiable). Uncle's specialties also include fresh blue crabs with Hunan wine sauce, seasonal sliced venison with garlic sauce, and frogs legs Hunan style. Uncle Tai's is one of a very few restaurants that offer the Chinese hot pot. This is a brass cylinder surrounded by a moat of boiling broth, in which you cook tidbits selected from a tray of meats and vegetables. Here they feature the chrysanthemum hot pot and the Yunnan steamer pot, a variant where chicken and dried scallops are steamed in an earthenware vessel. Sesame banana is a lovely variation on the usual caramelized fruit, cracked by dipping it into ice water to create a crunchy-soft texture. Adventurous dinners will cost about $14 per person.

UNCLE TAI'S HUNAN YUAN, 1059 Third Avenue, Manhattan. Telephone: (212) TE8-0850. Hours: 12-11, daily. Cards: AE, DC. Reservations suggested. Free parking after 6 pm. Full bar service.

Frog's Legs Hunan Style	8.75
Fresh Blue Crabs w. Hunan Wine Sauce	8.75
Shredded Chicken w. Beansprouts	9.25
Sliced Duck w. Young Ginger Root	9.25
Uncle Tai's Beef	11.25
Sauteed Sliced Pheasant (seasonal)	9.25
Chunked Rabbit w. Orange Flavor	9.25
Sliced Venison w. Garlic Sauce (Seasonal)	9.50
Beggar's Hunan Ham	8.75
Dry-Sauteed Shredded Beef Hunan Style	8.75
Sliced Lamb Hunan Style	8.75
Special Hunan Vegetable Pie	8.75
Chunked Chicken w. Pineapple	8.75
Sa-Chia Shrimp	8.95
Sauteed Beef, Hunan Style	8.95
Uncle Tai's Tri-Color Lobster	19.75
Quick Sauteed Jumbo Shrimp	11.25

Manhattan: Upper East Side
VASATA
Czechoslovakian $

A Czech restaurant originally opened at this location back in 1890. Then in 1959 the Vasatas took over and remodelled, giving the place the atmosphere of a cozy tavern. It is easy to feel at home in the low-ceilinged room with wooden beams and plain walls, where the staff serves pleasantly and informally. The menu has recently changed from complete dinners to à la carte, with entrée prices now ranging from $2.95 for dumplings with eggs to $8.95 for crisp duckling or $9.95 for veal à la Vasata (sautéed veal with duck livers and bacon). Everything is substantial and prepared in good home style under the direction of Mrs. Vasata. Many of the main dishes are made to order and require 25 minutes to prepare—a worthwhile wait easily shortened by some of the great Czech beer or one of the modestly priced wines. Soups are sturdy, dumplings solid but tasty, and of course desserts include the famous *palacinky,* thin pancakes filled with apricot jam or chocolate sauce. You can add a dimension to these by having them flamed in cognac for $1.35 extra.

VASATA, 339 East 75th Street, Manhattan. Telephone: (212) 650-1686. Hours: 5-10, Monday; until 11, Tuesday-Saturday; 12-10, Sunday. Cards: AE, MC. Reservations suggested. Parking in nearby garage. Full bar service.

Roast Long Island Duckling à la Vasata	8.95
Roast Loin of Pork	7.95
Roast Chicken	6.85
Chicken with Paprika Cream sauce	6.85
POT ROAST ESTERHAZY	
(cream sauce with thinly sliced vegetables)	7.95
VEAL IN PAPRIKA CREAM SAUCE	6.25
DUCK LIVERS. Bacon and Browned Onions. with Wine Sauce	5.95
Chicken Livers in Brown Sauce	4.95
Smoked Beef Tongue	6.55
Cheese or Ham Omelet	3.55
Fresh Calf's Brain with Eggs	4.55
Dumplings with Eggs	2.95

*Breaded Fresh Calf's Brain	6.85
*Chopped Veal Steak (breaded and deep fried)	3.95
*Natur Schnitzel	8.95
*Wiener Schnitzel	8.95
*Schnitzel Cordon Bleu	9.55
*Breaded Pork Chops	8.95
*Pork Chops Serbien (with onions, green peppers, tomatoes)	8.95
*Shish-Kebab (pork tenderloin, tomatoes, onions, green peppers and bacon)	8.95
*Mixed Grill (pork, veal, beef, duck livers and ham)	9.95
*Escalopes of Veal à la Vasata (veal sauté in butter with duck livers and bacon)	9.95
*Fillet Mignon, vegetable garnish	9.95
*Beef Fillet with Wine sauce and Browned onions	8.95
*Breaded Fried Chicken	8.95

*Please allow 25 minutes for preparation

Manhattan: Wall Street Area
WINDOWS ON THE WORLD
CELLAR IN THE SKY
International $$$

The World Trade Center is a Manhattan must whether or not one dines there. The WTC stands on the site of the gone but never-to-be-forgotten Washington Market, and a spirit of high living abounds in more than the vertical sense. On the ground floor there are fast-food nooks and the Market Bar and Dining Rooms, where the menu, marked up daily with fresh specials, reads better than it tastes. Towering 107 floors above is Windows on the World Restaurant and its Cellar in the Sky. The view of lower Manhattan from any of the great window walls is breathtaking. The main dining room operates as a private dining club for lunch; non-members must pay a $7.50 surcharge for admittance. Better to fly up to the bar for a drink and a look, then descend to dine elsewhere. At night, the dining room becomes public and offers dinners at $18.50 that include such main dishes as *coulibiac* of salmon; local duckling roasted crisp and served with three purées; and shrimp in wine and cream with fresh grapes. À la carte grills begin at $10.50. These prices do not include wine, but wine is the real reason to spend money here. There is a handsome card that lists bottles from Argentina through Yugoslavia, at prices scarcely more than they sell for in a wine shop. But that is only a beginning: Ask for the *full* wine list and you get 15 full pages, packed with astonishing bargains (Yugoslavian Cabernet, $3.25) or mighty majesties (Château Mouton-Rothschild 1934, $128). Winemaster Kevin Zraly, who assembled this monument, is a genius.

The Stendahl Choice at Windows is unquestionably the section called Cellar in the Sky. Dinners only are served at $45 per person. There is no choice, but the foods are among the best offered at Windows, and with your meal

DINNER

Turban of Sole in Aspic
Vegetable Pâté, Tomato Frappé
Nearby Clams and Oysters
Melon and Fresh Ginger
Croustade of Chicken Livers, Béarnaise

or

Spinach Consommé with Dumplings
Corn and Crab Soup
Cream of Carrot — Iced

Coulibiac of Salmon
Poached Chicken with Tomatoes and Saffron, Julia
Roast Prime Sirloin, Braised Celery, Sauce Périgourdine
Local Duckling Roasted Crisp, Three Purées
Shrimp in White Wine and Cream with Green Grapes

Three Green Salad

The Golden Lemon Tart	Chocolate Pastry Cake
Strawberry Bavarian Cream	Kiwi Fruit Parfait
Apple Sorbet	Ice Creams — Best of Brands

Colombian Coffee	Tea Selection

$18.50

you will receive five wines adventurously selected from five different countries. (The wines alone ordinarily would cost more than $45.) A typical evening starts with a Fino Sherry, continues with a California Pinot Chardonnay, an estate-bottled Bordeaux, an Italian Gattinara, and finishes with a Moet & Chandon Demi Sec Champagne. A typical menu includes Spanish chorizo, mushroom consommé, *moussaka à la Turque,* saddle of veal, fresh fennel salad, international cheeses and a *poire soufflé glacé.* Best of all, wines and menu are changed twice a month.

WINDOWS ON THE WORLD RESTAURANT, 107th Floor, World Trade Center, Manhattan. Telephone: (212) 938-1111. Membership club lunch: Monday-Friday. Main dining room open to public: 5-10, Monday-Saturday; grand buffet, 12-3, Saturday-Sunday. Cellar in the Sky: one dinner sitting at 7:30, Monday-Saturday. Cards: AE, BA/Visa, CB, DC, MC. Reservations should be made well in advance. Free parking for dinner guests in World Trade Center garage. Full bar service.

Manhattan: Greenwich Village
YE WAVERLY INN
American $

At the corner of Bank Street and Waverly Place, in an area that still has memories of Colonial times, Ye Waverly Inn has quietly flourished, and fed several generations of diners who like good plain American food at good plain prices. Decor is cozy, with working fireplaces, wooden booths and candlelight, in a house that seems almost as much a home as a commercial enterprise. The little menu lists nine complete dinners, all of them $9.50 or less, with the least expensive only $6.95. Main dishes at lunch, with two vegetables plus either a soup or a dessert, are a mere $4.50 for down-home cooking like roast stuffed duck with applesauce or Southern fried chicken. Dinner offers choices such as the "big deal," a grilled shell steak with French fried onion rings; or calf's liver, broiled fresh fish or a satisfyingly old-fashioned individual chicken potpie. Desserts include warm pecan pie, a cake of the day or hot fruit cobbler à la mode. House bar specials include such gaudy items as grasshoppers and pink squirrels made with vanilla ice cream; they also serve real drinks. For good vittles at yesterday's prices, Ye Waverly Inn cannot be beat.

YE WAVERLY INN, 16 Bank Street, Manhattan. Telephone: (212) WA9-4377. Lunch: 11:45-2, Tuesday-Saturday. Dinner: 5:15-10, Monday-Thursday; until 11, Friday-Saturday; 4:30-9, Sunday. Sunday brunch: 12-3:30. Cards: AE, DC, MC. Reservations suggested. Street parking. Full bar service

Manhattan: Midtown East
ZAPATA'S
Mexican $

Most Mexican restaurants in New York are frauds. Caribbean cooking, so often found here, is not Mexican. (In Mexico rice is dry and lightly spiced, not wet and yellow-colored.) And the commercial taco shells used by most restaurants taste secondhand and lifeless. Zapata's is an exception. The exterior is so disreputable you might think it was closed down. Inside, the narrow, rather dim room is not romantic either. What does that matter? Seated at your small table you await true Mexican cooking by a chef who knows the authentic cuisine. Nachos, crisp little tortilla chips with melted cheese and a disc of hot jalapeño pepper, are superior as an appetizer. Ceviche is the only untraditional item, based on shrimp instead of the more customary marinated raw fish. Carefully prepared regional specialties include *mole verde,* chicken with green sauce and ground pumpkin seeds, and *mole poblano,* chicken with that lip-smacking sauce compounded of various chiles, ground nuts and bitter chocolate. This is also the only restaurant I know that occasionally serves the great Mexican delicacy, *cabrito* (baby goat). As usual in a Mexican restaurant, best buys are the combination plates. They include assemblies of such items as tacos (with the tortillas fried to order), tamales, burritos and enchiladas. The latter are particularly good here. If you want a mild dish, order them *Suiza* (Swiss-style)—with a light green sauce and a dollop of sour cream on top. Combination plates are $6.25; entrées with refried beans and rice are $4.95 to $7.95. Fine Mexican beer (Carta Blanca and Dos Equis) are *the* quaff with spicy Mexican foods.

ZAPATA'S, 330 East 53rd Street, Manhattan. Telephone: (212) 223-9408. Hours: 12-3, 5-11, Monday-Friday; 5-11, Saturday-Sunday. Cards: AE, BA/Visa, MC. Reservations not necessary. Street parking. Full bar service.

MEXICAN SPECIALTIES*

TACOS - chicken or beef	4.95
ENCHILADAS - chicken, cheese, or beef	4.95
TOSTADAS - chicken or beef	4.95
TAMALES - beef	4.95
MOLE PABLANO - chicken in mole sauce	5.95
MOLE VERDE - chicken in green mole sauce	5.95
SWISS ENCHILADAS - chicken enchiladas marinated in green sauce	5.75
CABRITO - baby goat monterey style	6.95
POLLO ala ZAPATA - chicken in a mild ranchero sauce	5.95
CARNE TAMPIQUENA - steak in ranchero sauce	7.95
CHILE RELLENO - stuffed green pepper with beef	5.95
BURRITOS - beef or chicken	5.95
FLAUTAS - rolled tacos, fried crisp	5.95

(All Entrees include a portion of Refried Beans and Rice)

New York City: Other Boroughs
The Bronx, Brooklyn and Queens

Brooklyn: Fulton and Front Streets, 1816.

The Bronx
IL BOSCHETTO
Italian
$$

Despite its name ("little grove"), this establishment stands in an area desperately in need of greenery. But don't let the improbable location prevent you from making an advance reservation, for this robust Italian delight stays open seven days a week and almost always plays to a full house. Plays is an apt word, for the members of the Diaferia family, who run the place, are like culinary Marx Brothers. They tablehop continuously, carrying on running conversations with guests while plunking down huge platters of superior food. There are pages of all the Italian classics on the menu, plus several inventions of the Diaferia family. I am proud that one creation (not on the menu) has been named *pasta alla lampara, Stendahl*. It's a hunger-stopping rhapsody of fettuccine, prosciutto, pimientos, Parmesan, squash, black olives, and a béchamel sauce that includes both cognac and Chablis. Mixed fish fry Neapolitan must be eaten to be believed; the fried zucchini is some of the best ever. And seafood, chicken and veal are all first-rate. As for a testimonial, I can think of none better than what the family says about itself: "Four brothers, one nephew, one cousin, and our great father. A team capable of running anything." I agree. Lunch may run as high as $12, dinners around $15.

IL BOSCHETTO, 1660 East Gun Hill Road, The Bronx. Telephone: (212) 379-9335. Hours: 11-10:30, Monday-Thursday; 11-midnight, Friday; 4:30-midnight, Saturday; 12:30-10, Sunday. Cards: AE, BA/Visa, CB, DC, MC. Reservations suggested. Valet parking. Full bar service.

Brooklyn
GAGE & TOLLNER
Seafood/Chops

$$

Back in 1884, when Brooklyn was a city separate from Manhattan, Mr. Gage and Mr. Tollner founded a restaurant that is apparently immortal. In 1889, G&T moved to its present location, and its original decor has been refurbished but never changed from that day. The dining room is tiny and narrow, made to look larger and more impressive by arched mirrors along the wall and across the rear. At night gaslights glow above the worn tables. Oyster crackers and beaten biscuits are still traditional adornments. Waiters wear hash marks on their sleeves, and a few have served hitches longer than the life spans of some customers. Food in recent years has been uneven, but Gage & Tollner's will wear a halo as long as its dusty doors remain open, and as long as its fish are glowing fresh. While the menu is heavy on sections such as oysters, bisques, crabmeat, soft clam bellies and other seafoods, there are also Welsh rabbits, omelettes, steaks, chops and other meats such as chicken à la Maryland, with bacon and corn fritters in cream sauce. There are 15 styles of potatoes, 14 salads and a separate menu for desserts and cordials. Perhaps the most famous dessert here is brandy Alexander pie. A rounded meal will be about $12 to $15 per person for lunch or dinner.

GAGE & TOLLNER, 372 Fulton Street, Brooklyn. Telephone: (212) 875-5181. Hours: 11:30-9, Monday-Friday; 4-11, Saturday; closed Sunday. Cards: AE, BA/Visa, DC, MC. Reservations suggested. Parking in nearby municipal garage. Full bar service.

Soft Clam Bellies

Belly Broil	6.25	Chicago	6.50
Milk Stew	6.50	Baltimore Fry	6.25
Cream Stew	6.75	Milk Broil	6.50
Fry	6.25	Celery Broil	6.50
Seasoned Fry	6.25	Cream Broil	6.75
Pan Roast	6.25	Shell Roast	6.25
Dewey Pan Roast	6.50	Celery Cream Broil	6.75
Steamed	6.25	Shell Roast (Casino)	6.25
Fritters	6.75	A la Newburg	6.75
Duxbury Stew	6.50	Fricaseed	6.50

Steaks, Chops, Other Meats

Sirloin Steak for 2	21.00	Single English Mutton Chop with Sausage, Bacon and Kidney	9.25
Single Sirloin Steak	11.50		
Filet Mignon	11.00		
Minute Steak	8.00	Calf's Liver and Bacon or Onions	6.75
Chopped Steak with Mushroom Caps	5.75	Broiled Ham Steak	6.50
Loin Lamb Chops (2)	10.50	Lamb Kidneys, En Brochette	5.25
Loin Lamb Chops with Bacon, Sausage and Kidney	11.25	Plain	5.25
Single Lamb Chop	5.75	Lamb Kidneys, Saute with Mushrooms in Gravy	6.00
Single English Mutton Chop	8.50		

French Fried Potatoes included with Steaks and Chops

Chicken

Fried with Bacon and Corn Fritters	6.50	Broiled or Fried	6.00
A la Maryland with Bacon and Corn Fritters (Cream Sauce)	6.75	Chicken Livers Saute with Mushrooms in Gravy	5.75
		Chicken Livers en Brochette	5.50
A la King	6.50	Club Sandwich	4.00
Chicken Sandwich	3.00		

Fresh Fish (*In Season*)

Bluefish Boned	5.50	Striped Bass Boned	8.50
Brook Trout	6.50	Fried Seafood Combination	7.50
Filet of Sole	5.50		
Halibut Steak	8.75	Seafood a la Newburg	10.50
Red Snapper	9.25	Seafood au Gratin	10.50
Lemon Sole	6.75	Seafood Salad	10.50
Salmon Steak	9.00	Swordfish	......
Boned Shad	......	Smelts	......
Shad Roe	......	Shad & Roe Combination	......

Brooklyn
PETER LUGER
Steakhouse

$$

For nearly 100 years Luger's has been serving meat and potatoes without frills. Although prices are inked in, because meat costs are so unstable, this famous steakhouse probably serves finer meat for less money than any other in New York. The menu is bare-bone simplicity (although all the bones here are mighty with meat). You see steak for one, two, three or four, a steak sandwich, double loin lamb chops and roast prime rib—when available. That is about the total listing for dinner. Lunches are more complex: Each day there are three specialties, and they adventurously include lamb stew and chicken. "Steak for Two," a single mammoth porterhouse with a filet mignon joined on the bone, is plenty for three hungry truckers. The lamb chops are Jim Brady size and great. Appetizers list no soups or salads, only a basic plate of thick red tomato slices with or without onion rings. With these, and everything else, comes "Luger's Own Sauce," a sweet-sharp, tomato-horseradish

---

Daily Luncheon Special

Served with Potato and Vegetable

Monday

1. ROAST PRIME RIBS OF BEEF 4.95
2. POT ROAST 3.95
3. CHOPPED STEAK, SMOTHERED ONIONS 2.95

Tuesday

1. ROAST PRIME RIBS OF BEEF 4.95
2. CHICKEN 3.95
3. KNOCKWURST AND SAUERKRAUT 2.95

condiment. French fries, the fat type, are the only item I do not care for here, but Luger's German-fried potatoes are a delicious crusty creation. Spinach is the usual vegetable offered. The art nouveau service plates are beautiful, but in general the decor is as spare as the menu: wood wall panels painted black, bare wood tables—just the way things looked in 1887, no doubt. Waiters are wise, in every sense of the term, and get your plates to the table piping hot thanks to a chiming alert system over the doorway. There is a brief wine list, but beer, Schaefer's or Beck's, is the drink for this simple and simply magnificent fare. Lunch entrées, with potato and vegetable, are $2.95 to $4.95. At dinner steaks average $13 per person with vegetables and potatoes à la carte. There is another Peter Luger in Great Neck, Long Island, but stick with the original.

PETER LUGER, 178 Broadway (foot of Williamsburgh Bridge), Brooklyn. Telephone: (212) 387-7400. Hours: 11:30-9:30, Monday-Thursday; until 11:15, Friday-Saturday; 1-9:30, Sunday. No credit cards. Reservations suggested. Street parking. Full bar service.

Wednesday

1. ROAST PRIME RIBS OF BEEF 4.95
2. BEEF STEW 3.95
3. CHOPPED STEAK, SMOTHERED ONIONS 2.95

Thursday

1. ROAST PRIME RIBS OF BEEF 4.95
2. CORNED BEEF AND CABBAGE 4.75
3. CORNED BEEF HASH .... 2.95   WITH EGG 3.75

Friday

1. ROAST PRIME RIBS OF BEEF 4.95
2. FRESH FISH IN SEASON 4.75
3. CORNED BEEF HASH .... 2.95   WITH EGG 3.75

Queens: Astoria
LA BOCCALETTA
Italian $

Just 15 minutes by subway from Carnegie Hall, Astoria is not generally sought out by gourmets from Manhattan, although its ethnic restaurants (chiefly Italian and Greek) have a lot to offer. La Boccaletta, "little wine pitcher," is a treat, specializing in first-rate pasta, authentic north Italian specialties and fresh vegetables generally touched with a bit of garlic and good olive oil. (Rumor has it the chef picks vegetables daily from his private garden on his way to work.) La Boccaletta is crowded by local businessmen at noon, but dining is leisurely at night. The owner-host, Severo, an experienced restaurateur from Trieste, knows how to satisfy customers. Ambience is informal, with little pottery boccalettas strung along the beams, and with fresh flowers on every table. A special not to be missed is *tortellini della nonna,* "the little meat-filled dumplings of my grandmother," cooked perfectly al dente. And apparently grandmama puts an individual fresh green pea in the navel of each of the little rings. Fantastic! They are proud here of their special veal in champagne sauce, but I prefer the various chicken dishes. You can have the best of both by ordering a veal and chicken combination. The zucchini fritti is a must, and is a bargain, too. The wine list offers a good range of Italian wines at fair prices. Consult Severo for his specials of the moment. Lunches are about $8.50, dinners about $12, depending on what you build from the à la carte menu.

LA BOCCALETTA, 33-05 Broadway, Astoria, Queens. Telephone: (212) 626-6900. Hours: 12-3, 4-11, Sunday-Thursday; until 11:30 Friday-Saturday; closed Monday. Cards: AE, BA/Visa, DC, MC. Reservations suggested. Street parking. Full bar service.

~ FISH ~

Scampi alla Veneziana or Fra Diavolo   7.75

Filet of Sole Belle Meuniere   5.75

Broiled Bass or Marechiaro   5.95

Calamari alla Luciana or Fra Diavolo   5.25

Baby Frogs Legs Prezzemolo   6.95

Special Sole with Baby Shrimps   6.25

~ ENTREES ~

Veal

Special Veal Champagne   6.75
Filet of Veal Marsala   6.25
Scaloppine of Veal Francese   5.95
Veal Piccata   5.95
Saltimbocca alla Romana   6.75
Veal Sorrentino   6.75
Veal alla Fiorentina   5.95
Veal alla Parmigiana (spaghetti)   5.75

Chicken

Chicken alla Triestina 5.25	Chicken Francese 5.25
Chicken alla Fiorentina 5.25	Chicken Mimosa 5.75
Chicken Sorrentino 5.75	Chicken Zingarella 5.75

Chicken Bolognese   5.75

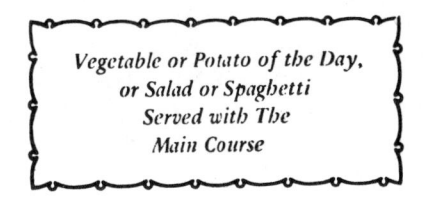

---

*Vegetable or Potato of the Day,
or Salad or Spaghetti
Served with The
Main Course*

Queens: Astoria
VILLA GAUDIO
Pizza

$

Until recently Villa Gaudio was a tiny bare-tabled pizza joint. But an expansion into larger quarters next door has transformed it into a handsome restaurant with raw red-brick walls, lustrous wooden beams, white tablecloths and attractive flatware. This new opulence was made possible by one humble product: pizza. For some 20 years Luigi Gaudio and his brother Frank have been dealing piping hot pizzas to a faithful clientele, who in the earliest days had to stand outside while the Gaudio brothers passed the pizza through a window. Later a little awning was erected to protect the patient customers who lined up, even in the rain. There are many family-run Italian restaurants in this Italian-Greek neighborhood, but there is only one undisputed pizza master, and it is the pizza that makes Villa Gaudio worth a pilgrimage. If you can catch Luigi in an unbusy moment, he may reveal to you the secrets of judging a proper pizza: If the crust contains any bubbles, it was baked too soon; when the dough is right, a wedge will not droop when lifted. The dough at Gaudio is a secret formula known only to Luigi and Frank. No other hand touches it until the brothers approve it for baking. All the usual pizza varieties are featured, plus one Dagwood staggerer with *everything* on it, The Gaudio Special. Prices are competitive ($2.70 to $6.50 for the pizzas), but can one really price a work of art?

VILLA GAUDIO, 4013 30th Avenue, Astoria, Long Island City. Telephone: (212) 721-2882. Hours: 11-midnight, daily. Cards: AE, BA/Visa, DC, MC. Reservations advised for parties of four or more at dinner. Parking in nearby lot. Full bar service.

Queens: Glendale
ZUM STAMMTISCH
German $

Little Germany is traditionally thought of as being along Manhattan's 86th Street, but there is a unique little German patch out on Long Island, a bit to the east and south of Forest Hills suburbia, named Glendale. It's a *gemütlich* neighborhood with several Old Country restaurants. One of the best is Zum Stammtisch, "your special table." Here you'll get honest German food without frills and without a big check; a full meal is $7 or even less. If there is a flaw, it is that even with a reservation you'll have to stand in line. Zum is small, its customers like to linger long and comfortably and no one tries to rush those seated. German is heard more often than English, even from youthful tables, and good steins of beer are more popular than martinis. The dining room is adorned simply, with a couple of mournful moose heads and some dark wood beams. The waitresses are friendly and patient, and the food is done in perfect family style without fuss. The menu remains unchanged, day or night. There is goulash soup, and appetizers include home-style head cheese and *ochesmaul salat* (thin slivers of ox tongue). Main dishes would warm the hearts of the Katzenjammer Kids and the Captain, and prices start as low as $3. Wienerschnitzel, sauerbraten and nearly everything else, including grilled bratwurst, comes with kraut, home fries or red cabbage, and servings are huge. The Stendahl Choice is *jagerschnitzel,* a spectacular platter of excellent veal, breaded and fried to a crunchy, puffy succulence, then topped with a thick brown gravy, bumpy with button mushrooms. Desserts should taste homemade but they do not. German wines worth exploring.

ZUM STAMMTISCH, 69-46 Myrtle Avenue, Glendale, Queens. Telephone: (212) 386-3014. Hours: 12-12, Sunday-Thursday; Until 1, Friday-Saturday. No credit cards. Reservations necessary. Street parking. Full bar service.

Queens: Rego Park
CAFE VALOIS
French $

Along Queens Boulevard, the main stem of Queens, there are countless pizza stands and knish-nosheries, but few worthwhile dining establishments. Despite Cafe Valois' prominent location across from bustling Alexander's department store, few shoppers seem to find it, and it is possible to dine here quietly and pleasantly. Authentically French in kitchen and in ambience, Cafe Valois offers excellent food for modest prices. The concern of the two waiters who serve with old-time professional skill suggests that they are the owners of this oasis in the pizza desert. Luncheons are $3.95 and up, and include a splendid potage, a choice of half-a-dozen carefully prepared entrées, beverage, and an interesting dessert. The dinner menu offers a wide à la carte selection, but also a complete meal for only $9.95. Again, there is a wide choice of items, including seven main dishes. Judging by its appearance on many tables, the house specialty seems to be duckling with cherry sauce and wild rice—and this favorite is among the items on the $9.95 dinner. Cheese soufflés are another standout, high, fluffy, moist. While vegetables are overcooked in the French manner, they are fresh and aswim with butter. A modest but thoughtful wine list is pleasantly priced with a few bottles as low as $6.

CAFE VALOIS, 95-96 Queens Boulevard, Rego Park, Queens. Telephone: (212) 896-6945. Hours: 12-2:30, 6-10:30, Monday-Friday; 5-11, Saturday; 4-10:30, Sunday; closed Monday. Cards: AE, BA/Visa, CB, DC, MC. Reservations necessary on weekends. Street parking. Full bar service.

The Environs of New York

Long Island, Westchester County, Putnam and Ulster Counties, Northern New Jersey

Rutherford, New Jersey, 1876.

Long Island: Bellerose
ARTURO'S
Italian $$

This is another of those fine restaurants in an impossible location. You can easily pass the place without seeing it, since the entrance is not large and the awning is almost hidden behind the marquee of a movie house next door. Parking is also next to impossible (look for a side street). So why bother? Because this is a house of quality and geniality, serving all the Italian favorites and a lot of family inventions besides. Two brothers run Arturo's, one who does tableside cooking, and one who rules the kitchen but somehow can't help bouncing out in his floppy white hat to table-hop among the guests. All food here is of fine quality, and the only complaint is that they apparently have never heard of saucers. Every item arrives piled high on a platter. Also, if you're an old customer, part of almost everything cooked at nearby tables finds its way to your table. An indication of the family inventiveness is the *torta primavera*. This is a dazzling appetizer built of crêpes, no less than 13 layers filled with mushrooms, salami, artichoke hearts, cheeses and other meats and vegetables. This astonishing construction is topped with a frosting of delicious homemade mayonnaise, then chilled and sliced like a birthday cake. Pasta dishes are sparked by sauces that include Nova Scotia lox and vodka, or bits of ham and cognac. Dishes that feature chicken or veal ($6.95 to $8.95) are better than good. All this does not come cheaply, but when ever have the good things of life been cheap?

ARTURO'S, 246-04 Jericho Turnpike (two blocks east of the Cross Island Parkway), Bellerose, Long Island. Telephone: (516) 352-7418. Hours: 12-2:30, 5-9:30, Monday-Thursday; until 11 pm, Friday and Saturday; 1-9, Sunday; closed Tuesday. Cards: AE, BA/Visa, CB, DC, MC. Reservations mandatory. Parking on side streets. Full bar service.

Farinacei (Pasta)

Spaghetti Gismondi . . . 6.00
Spaghetti Carbonara . . . 5.50
Rigatoni Scogliosi . . . 5.50
Paglia e Fieno 5.50
Tortellini Bolognese . . . 5.50

Mustaccioli Cognac . . . 6.00
Cannelloni 5.00
Linguine...white or red clam sauce 5.00
Fettuccine Alfredo 5.50
Tagliatelle Arturo 5.00

Pesci (Fish)

Broiled Lobster Tails . . 11.95
Lobster Tail Fradiavolo . 11.95
Stuffed Lobster Tails . . 12.95
Shrimp Marinara 7.95
Shrimp Scampi 7.95
Shrimp Parmigiana . . . 7.95
Shrimp Gratinate 7.95

Live Lobster from tank broiled ½ lb. . . 11.95
Live Lobster from tank fradiavolo . . 11.95
Stuffed Live Lobster from tank . . . 12.95
Lobster tail Fiorentina 8.00
Fresh Fillet Sole Broiled-white wine . 6.50
Fresh Bass Bonne Femme 6.75
Fresh Trout Meuniere 6.75

Zuppa Di Pesce . . 11.00

Vitello (Veal)

Veal Scaloppina Arturo 8.95
Veal Scaloppina Piccata 8.95
Veal Scaloppina Marsala Mushrooms 8.95
Veal Scaloppina Pizzaiola . . . 8.95
Lombatine Modenese 8.50
Veal Cutlet Cortina 7.50

Long Island: West Hempstead and Cedarhurst
CHEONG'S GARDEN-CHI LING GOURMET
Chinese $

Cheong's Garden of West Hempstead and Chi Ling of Cedarhurst are both operated by Francis Cheong and family. Although they are some distance from Manhattan, and despite Chi Ling's being tucked away behind JFK airport, both restaurants are near the pinnacles of quality, friendliness and service. Except for a few dishes (and several are the same under different poetic names), the two menus are identical, and prices likewise. The chief difference is that at Cheong's Garden, friendly, gentle Mrs. Cheong will greet you, and at Chi Ling, friendly gentle Francis Cheong will take care of you. Chi Ling is also the handsomer place. Along with traditional Szechwan, Hunan and Peking favorites—all prepared with finesse—inventive Mr. Cheong serves his own special dishes that tantalize with their delicacy and uniqueness of texture and taste. Cheong has a sophisticated background in all five of the Chinese cuisines. He is very articulate in English and explains and describes helpfully. Delights at both restaurants are too numerous to detail, but the Stendahl Choice at Chi Ling is unquestionably Governor Jo's duck, boneless duck that is breaded in lotus flour, twice-cooked, and served crunchily crisp in a light black bean sauce—a superb blend of textures and taste. A similar dish served at Cheong's Garden is called Cheong's Chicken, but I much prefer the darker taste of duck. Prosperity beef is a dish Cheong invented for a Chinese New Year banquet, but which will be supplied on order (not on the menus). This is a piquant but not blistery mélange of thinly sliced beef, bamboo shoots, bits of cabbage and a thick, slightly peppery sauce. Spectacular is the word for the special cold appetizer platter, "four delicacy." This comes as if ready to be photographed for a food magazine—tissue-thin slices of chicken breast are folded into an amazing resemblance to a white rose, surrounded by several kinds of seasoned meats, between rows of cold marinated-vegetable slivers. Seafood gets special treatment, and only the freshest fish is used. Chairman Mao's shrimp is the Stendahl Choice among seafoods, this being succulent fresh shrimp in a sauce of Chinese wine, garlic and mysteries that give it a faintly tart-sweet, truly indescribable taste. Dumplings and the homemade Shanghai spring rolls have the thinnest of wrappings. Everything, in fact, is recommended at either establishment. Dinner selections range from $4.75 to $9.95; lunch from $2.25 to $6.95.

CHEONG'S GARDEN, 190 Hempstead Turnpike, West Hempstead, Long Island. Telephone: (516) 292-1650. CHI LING GOURMET, 530 Central Avenue, Cedarhurst, Long Island. Telephone: (516) 295-2966. Hours for both restaurants: 12-11, Sunday-Thursday; until 12 pm, Friday and Saturday. Cards: AE, BA/Visa. DC, MC. Reservations suggested. Parking in rear. Full bar service.

~~~~~~

Gwo-Bar with Triple Delight **6.25**
Baby Shrimp, Sliced Chicken and Pork with Mushrooms, Water Chestnuts and Bamboo Shoots, Simmered in a Blended Mandarin Sauce and Served with a Sizzling Rice Cake.

Egg Plant Family Style **4.75**
Chunks of Egg Plant with Fresh Genger, Garlic, Scallions and Delicately Simmered in a Spicy Hunan Sauce.

Cheong's Garden Steak **8.50**
Thick Sliced Prime Filet of Beef with a touch of Chef's own Light Sweet and Sour Sauce.

Chairman Mao's Shrimp **6.50**
Jumbo Shrimp Sauteed with Scallion, Ginger, Chinese Rice Wine and touch of Garlic in a very Light Mandarin Sweet and Sour Sauce.

Chef's Amazing Beef **6.25**
Slice Prime Filet of Beef, with Black Mushroom, Bamboo Shoots and Snow Peas, Delicately Sauteed in our Chef's Secret Sauce.

Long Island: Port Washington
LA GOLETTA
Northern Italian $$

La Goletta means "little boat," and though you don't need sea legs to dine here, the view from the dockside windows is fascinating during the day and romantic by night. On weekends, when customers overflow to the second story of this small restaurant, the view is even better from higher up through a wall-long window. The decor is cozier, however, on the main floor where fire-burnt brick walls, low ceilings and fresh flowers add up to a country inn look. The pleasantness is increased by attentive and friendly service. The menu is chiefly northern Italian, with a few French touches. Among the appetizers, mussels marinière is a novel and delicious choice: Fresh mussels are heaped high in a soup plate over a delicious cream and chive sauce that is almost like a warm vichysoisse. Pastas are all carefully prepared and good. Although it is not listed, risotto may be ordered if the kitchen is not too busy. It is worth coming early for this dish, which may be ordered either with saffron or with *porcini* (superb wild Italian mushrooms). An excellent choice of entrée is breast of chicken *paesana*, moist boneless white meat, lightly breaded, in a delicate tomato-wine-herb sauce. While the veal *saltimbocca* is not my favorite because of a too-thick glaze, most other veal dishes are good. There are also daily specials, generally worth ordering. Desserts are homemade and outstanding, particularly the fudgy, well-liqueured "cake" called chocolate velvet. Lunches begin at $4.50; à la carte dinners average $15. Pleasant wine list.

LA GOLETTA, 57 Shore Road, Port Washington, Long Island. Telephone: (516) 883-2111. Hours: 12-3, 6-10, Tuesday-Friday; 6-11, Saturday; 4-10, Sunday; closed Monday. Cards: AE, BA/Visa, CB, DC, MC. Reservations suggested. Parking lot. Full bar service.

Scampi Goletta 9.50
Filet of Sole Meunière 7.25   Bay Scallops Provençale 8.75
                              Broiled Red Snapper with Bearnaise
                                                        Sauce 9.50
        Dover Sole Amandine 9.50

        Breast of Chicken Havana 7.50
Breast of Chicken Fiorentina 7.50
                              Duckling a l' Orange Flambé
                                with Wild Rice For Two 17.00

Broiled Sirloin Steak 10.95   Filet Mignon au Poivre 12.50
Broiled Filet Mignon 10.95   Filetto di Manzo Tiggiola 10.50
        Skillet Steak with Onions and Peppers 11.50

Chateaubriand Bouquetiere with Bearnaise Sauce - For Two 23.50

Rack of Lamb Garni - For Two 22.00

Vitello alla Parmigiana 8.25   Veal Picata al Limone 8.25
Veal Scaloppine Fratelli Funghi 8.50 Veal Scaloppine alla Bolognese 8.50
        Veal Saltimbocca 8.50

Long Island: Amityville
LA MANSARDE
French/Italian $$

Quite a way out on Long Island there is a strange but delightful stretch that harbors several fine restaurants within a mile of each other. La Mansarde stands out because of its ambition and its very pretty owner-chef, Rose Albano, who runs her establishment adventurously from a base of sound kitchen knowledge. Her menus are complicated. There is one for weeknights and Sunday dinner, a special Saturday menu with different items and higher prices altogether, a luncheon menu and yet another menu for Sunday brunch. Rose also has special holiday festivals and champagne dinners. All the menus are *table d'hôte* and include soup, salad, entrée, vegetable, a selection from the pastry cart and beverage. At Sunday brunch, entrées range from *quiche maison* or an omelette at $5.50 to lobster tails and shrimps Parisienne or sliced filet mignon in Madeira sauce at $7.95. For lunch, you may choose leg of lamb at $4.95 or one of the more expensive items at $6.50—broiled shrimp in garlic butter or calf's liver with brown sauce, onions and bacon. Weeknight dinners range from $8.50 to $14.25 for "steak Diane, a classic! Ask for a description." The menu for Saturday, the expensive night, is reproduced on the next page. Whenever Rose offers the rabbit casserole, order it. This delectable dish, the Stendahl Choice, is sealed with mustard-spread bread and baked, and then the bread is mashed to thicken a heady sauce. The large dessert trolley is attractive to look at, but too full of calories.

LA MANSARDE, 348 Merrick Road, Amityville, Long Island. Telephone: (516) 691-6881. Hours: 12-3, 6-10, daily; Sunday brunch. Cards: AE, BA/Visa, CB, DC. Reservations required. Parking lot. Full bar service.

Includes: Soup du Jour, Salad, Entrée, Vegetable

Bass Livornese 13.25
Sauce of crushed tomato
onions, garlic, olives, capers

Stuffed Sole 13.50
Baked. Lobster, scallops
shrimp stuffing

Snapper Amandine 13.25
Sauteed in lemon, butter
finished with toasted almonds

Filet of Sole 12.25
In a batter. Sauteed in
lemon, butter and white wine

Shrimp Scampi 14.75
Broiled shrimp in garlic
and butter sauce

Crêpe Mansarde 12.95
Parisian crepe stuffed with
seafood topped with mornay

Chicken Kiev 11.95
Rolled chicken
breast, herb butter stuffing

Veal Smyetana 12.25
Breaded cutlet, layers of ham
Gruyere cheese, sour cream

Duckling, Roasted 13.50
Choice of:
orange sauce or cherry sauce

Veal Cordon Bleu 13.95
Rolled cutlet stuffed with
ham & cheese

Veal Piccata 12.25
Thin slices of veal in
a lemon butter sauce

Leg of Lamb 12.25
Roasted. A hint of garlic
served in natural juices

Veal Marsala 13.25
Tender slices of veal
Marsala wine sauteed mushrooms

Steak Romano 14.95
Topped with a glaze of
garlic, tomato sauce, romano cheese

Steak au Poivre 14.95
Sauteed in a brown sauce
with pepper corns, brandy

Roquefort Steak 14.95
Broiled. In a sauce of white
wine and Roquefort cheese

Sliced Filet Mignon 14.95
Choice of marsala and mushrooms
or Bordelaise: a brown wine sauce

Filet Mignon Bearnaise 15.95
Broiled. Topped with a sauce
of hollandaise with Tarragon

Pastry Cart Selection, Coffee or Tea

Long Island: East Hills
L'ENDROIT
French

$$

L'Endroit means "The Place," a name that sets the tone for this establishment's pretension toward elegance. The food is excellent French, with all the favorites, plus a few house specialties. The kitchen understands *haute cuisine*. The ambience is warm—gleaming chandeliers, French kitchen utensils on the walls, a pastry wagon that excites hunger as you pass it by. "The Place" is small, however, and tables are packed too closely together. Specify that you do not want a table in the middle of the room, a crowded area where waiters are apt to bump your elbow when your fork is in mid-air. On jampacked weekends, L'Endroit is full of sound and fury; midweek it is filled more with excellent meats, well-seasoned sauces and fresh vegetables imaginatively served. They do very well by fish here, and duckling is a bit out of the ordinary, cooked with prunes and spirits. Desserts are almost maddeningly good; dieters simply must surrender to fluffy *gâteau Saint-Honoré* with its crispy pastry and creamy interior, or dense sweet chocolate cake, or whatever homemade specials flirt from the trolley. The menu is à la carte with dishes at luncheon ranging from $3.95 to $8.50, and main dishes at night ranging from $7.95 for frogs legs to $12.75 for a generous steak *au poivre grande champagne*.

L'ENDROIT, 148 Glen Cove Road, East Hills, Long Island. Telephone: (516) 621-6630. Hours: 12-2:30, 5-10, Monday-Thursday; until 11, Friday-Saturday; closed Sunday. Cards: AE, BA/Visa, CB, DC, MC. Reservations suggested. Parking lot. Full bar service.

Les Entrées

Tournedos Saint-Denis   12.75
Tournedos Bercy   11.50
Le Poulet sauté Pompadour   8.25
Supreme de Volaille Gismonda   8.00
Caneton aux Pruneaux a L'Eau-de-Vie   9.50
Les Grenouilles du Chef   7.95
Filet de Sole Murat   8.75
Les Scampis   10.00
La Cote de Veau Bouchère   11.25
Escalopes de Veau Zingara   8.95
Noisettes de Veau Chasseur   9.25
Les Ris de Veau Xérès   7.95

Specialtiés:

Le Foie de Veau Bercy   8.75
Le Steak au Poivre Grande Champagne   12.75
La Combination Parisienne   11.95

Long Island: Montauk
THE LITTLE PARK
Eclectic

$$

Classic cuisine is to be admired, but there is also a great deal to be said for the man who creates his own, taking from the world as he knows it some of the best and most tantalizing offerings and presenting them to the public over his personal signature. Such a restaurant is The Little Park, founded by a man who has roved the world and gleaned from many cultures recipes that he has refined and now presents in his own style. Tony Pan consolidates treasures from his travels and serves them forth in a delightful cross-culture menu. His wife makes the ice cream and sews the drapes, doing her thing in a most personal, and laudable, kind of enterprise. Hard to find, but worth searching for is The Little Park, which is so good it seems out of place in an area where most restaurants are either pizza parlors or seafood stands. The owner-chef puts his stamp on every dish he creates, beginning with an incredible taste treat humbly called spinach soup. This contains, in addition to spinach, puréed broccoli, chicken stock and cream, made perky with coriander and a zip of cayenne. Each specialty

Filet of sole muniere w/ aioli 8.50

Bifteck Marchand de Vins
  sautéed shell steak in wine-shallot butter sauce

Shrimp Romano 8.75
  - in shallots dry sherry heavy cream

Chicken curry Bombay 8.75
  w/ saffron rice

likewise benefits from the personal touch: Shrimps come afloat in a sauce of clams, well-scented with shallots and white wine. An unusual pasta dish, *Malagueña,* features piping hot spaghetti dressed in an uncooked sauce of chopped pine nuts, cheese, parsley, olive oil and more than whiff of garlic. Desserts are special, with a masterly mousse from the hand of Mrs. Pan that is deeply chocolate without being bitter, smooth and creamy—in short a master of mousses. Cassata is the classic dessert of Sicily, something between an ice cream pie and a cheese cake. Mr. Pan creates his from his own memories. Good. The entire menu changes, depending on the whims and most recent travels of the energetic, imaginative hosts. Service is informal. Decent wines are available at prices that make them attractive. This is food with a spark, in a faraway location. Dinner entrées average $8.75.

THE LITTLE PARK, South Elmwood and Emery Street, Montauk, Long Island. Telephone: (516) 668-3131. Hours: Thursday-Sunday, March-June 15; daily June 15-October 15. Cards: AE, BA/Visa. Reservations suggested. Parking lot. Full bar service.

Shrimp Catalan — 8.75
— in red wine, tomatoes sage-coriander flavored sauce

Tripe Chiana — 7.25
— in red wine, tomatoes flavored w/ Italian sausage

Veal Kidneys Montagnards — 8.50
— sautéed in butter w/ dry sherry shallots sweet cream

Long Island: Glen Cove
VILLA PIERRE
French

$$

Once an Italian restaurant of uneven reputation, Villa Pierre has risen to a superlative French establishment. One cannot call Villa Pierre new: The crooked little bar area leans that way because of age. The restaurant encompasses one of Long Island's oldest structures, supposedly a Hessian soldier outpost built during the Revolutionary War. In this truly professional restaurant, the kitchen turns out excellent food and the waiters are efficient, yet human. It would be unthinkable to hear that lamentable cry: "Who gets the veal?" For dinner there is a wide range of outstanding choices. I have enjoyed every dish sampled here, and admired the beauty of the presentation. Soups are superior and, best of all, served in heated bowls with second helpings kept warm on a serving table. There are nicely presented fresh fish from $8.75 to $11.50, and poultry and meat entrées from $8.25. The Stendahl Choice is *l'escalope de veau princesse,* white veal cutlet in a mouth-watering cream and cognac sauce. Vegetables are original and lightly cooked. Desserts are sinful, with a devastating winner in a chocolate mocha torte of airy dough, lusciously chocolatey and topped with chocolate sheets buttered with marzipan. The chief fault to find with Villa Pierre is its woefully uninspired wine list. Dinners average $18; lunch is considerably less expensive (average of $8), but the menu is less impressive.

VILLA PIERRE, Glen Cove Road, Glen Cove, Long Island. Telephone: (516) 671-2890. Hours: 12-3, 6-11, Tuesday-Friday; 6-11, Saturday; 4-10, Sunday; closed Monday. Cards: AE, BA/Visa. Reservations suggested. Valet parking. Full bar service.

Les Poissons

DELICE DE SOLE BREVAL — 8.50
poached filet of sole, white wine, sauce

CREVETTES BRAISEES GISELLE — 10.50
braised shrimps with garlic, clams and, bacon

CRABES SAUTES AMANDINE — 10.25
soft shell crabs (in season)

LA SOLE ANGLAISE SAUTE MEUNIERE — 11.50
English sole saute in butter

LE FILET DE ROUGET GRILLE — 10.25
broiled red snapper

LES CUISSES DE GRENOUILLE PROVENCALE — 8.75
frog legs saute in butter and garlic

HOMARD GRILLE
Broiled lobster according to market

LE LOUP DE MER BRAISE VILLA PIERRE — 8.95
braised stripe bass, fine herbs, and white wine

LE ROUGET EN PAPILLOTE — 9.95
filet of red snapper baked in paper bag

LA TRUITE SAUTEE BELLE MEUNIERE — 8.75
fresh brook trout saute with Mushrooms

Les Viandes

LE SUPREME DE CHAPON CORDON BLEU — 7.75
breast of chicken stuffed with ham and cheese

LE POUSSIN EN CASSEROLE MASCOTTE — 8.50
roast squab chicken mushrooms and artichoke

LE PAILLARD DE VEAU EUGENE — 9.95
veal cutlet with crab meat and asparagus spears

L'ESCALOPE DE VEAU PRINCESSE — 8.95
veal cutlet, cream and cognac sauce

LE FOIE DE VEAU SAUTE LYONNAISE — 8.25
calf liver saute, onions

L'ESCALOPE DE VEAU SAUTE BEURRE ET CIRRON — 8.75
veal cutlet saute in butter and lemon

LE CANETON POELE A L'ORANGE (For Two) — 19.00
roast duckling, orange sauce with wild rice

LE STEAK FLAMBE AU POIVRE VERT — 12.25
steak flambe with green pepper corns

LES MIGNONETTES DE BOEUF BORDELAISE — 11.50
sliced filet mignon, red wine sauce

LE CHATEAUBRIAND BEARNAISE (For Two) — 24.75
double broil filet mignon served garni

Long Island: Glen Cove
RESTAURANT ZANGHI
Continental

$$$

Restaurants outside Manhattan too often suffer from inconsistency, being great on Tuesdays and ragged on Thursdays. A beautiful exception is Restaurant Zanghi, perhaps as the result of experience and training: Father Zanghi, a former chef for the Italian Lines, and son Zanghi began their restaurant careers as boys doing menial chores in the kitchen. The sophisticated, seasonal menu is basically French with an Italian accent. Soups are memorable, and among the appetizers the eggplant Siciliana is a silky tantalizer. All pastas are superior, and the fettuccine with white truffles, when in season, will remind you of the best restaurants in Milano. Zanghi's is more expensive than an ordinary restaurant for good reason: Poultry is obtained fresh-killed, veal is cream-white and fork-tender, and sauces are outstanding. A Stendahl Choice is the duck Smitane, featuring a totally fat-free, tender duck with crisp skin, laved in a sour cream and wine sauce approaching the sublime. Desserts are fabulous, one and all. The Zanghi wine cellar matches the best in Manhattan. Few restaurants anywhere, even in Italy, stock that rare Italian treat Brunello di Montalcino, but Zanghi offers two. And many a good West Coast restaurant stocks fewer California wines. For dinner, without wine, count at least $18 per person.

RESTAURANT ZANGHI, 50 Forest Avenue, Glen Cove, Long Island. Telephone: (516) 759-0900. Lunch: 12-2:30, Monday-Friday. Dinner: 6-10, Monday-Thursday; until 10:30, Friday-Saturday; 4-9:30, Sunday. Cards: AE, BA/Visa, CB, DC, MC. Reservations suggested. Parking lot. Full bar service.

Putnam County: North Brewster
THE ARCH
Continental $$

The menu here exists only on a blackboard and in the chef-owner's mind. Dishes are mostly descended from classic French cuisine, but each has a special name and a special touch bestowed by a loving, creative cook. Everything I have tasted has been beyond reproach. The Arch has been attracting loyal fans for a long time, but it is new at the North Brewster address. This former residence still has the charm of a country home—open fireplace, intimate lighting, spaciousness, and, above all, a staff that really tries to turn customers into guests. The changing menu forever offers surprising touches, reminiscent of the way French-Swiss play with the French cuisine. A couple of illustrations: *escalope de veau Monte Carlo* is a milky veal cutlet sautéed with oysters in a light cream sauce, topped with Gruyère cheese and popped under the broiler to glaze. Sole Riche is a tender filet poached, then stuffed with spinach, before being napped with a cream sauce chunky with nuggets of scallops and lobster meat. A typical dessert is a puffy soufflé, either chocolate or Grand Marnier, dressed with a delicate sauce sabayon. There are many original choices on the $18.50 *prix fixe* dinner. The wine list is a good one. Locals throng the snug, clublike little bar, warm with gentle light and polished woods.

THE ARCH; Route 22, North Brewster, Putnam County, New York. Telephone: (914) 279-5011. Hours: 6-10, Wednesday-Sunday; closed Monday-Tuesday. Cards: AE, BA/Visa, MC. Reservations requested. Valet parking. Full bar service.

Westchester County: Scarsdale
BARTHOLOMEW'S
American $

Imagine sipping cocktails in an upstairs back room delightfully overfurnished in a Dickensian manner. Imagine dining beneath spreading ferns hanging from a 40-foot ceiling, waited upon by young ladies in fluted white caps and trailing dresses. Imagine good plain food served in such surroundings where the bill will probably be less than $25 for two diners. An oddity about Bartholomew's is that they offer no soups, appetizers or vegetables. Instead, with each à la carte entrée you have a choice of three copious salads of different types. Main dishes are surprisingly inexpensive and generally of good quality. A man-sized, juicy New York sirloin is only $7.25, and a solid slab of tender roast beef—crusty outside or pink center cut, your choice—is even cheaper. There are many daily specials not on the menu, most of them fish or seafood, all at uniformly gentle prices. Desserts do not inspire awe, and the wine list is a downright disgrace. Still, with nostalgic decor, friendly staff and those good low prices, Bartholomew's is definitely worth a visit.

BARTHOLOMEW'S, 2 Weaver Street, Scarsdale, New York. (One mile from Exit 21 of the Hutchinson Parkway.) Telephone: (914) 725-3900. Hours: 11:30-2:30, 5:30-10, Monday-Thursday; until 11, Friday and Saturday; 1-4, Sunday brunch. Cards: AE, BA/Visa. Reservations not accepted. Parking lot. Full bar service.

Dinner Fare

All entrees are served with a baked potato and your choice of Bartholomew's Salad.

Ribs of Beef – cooked in the traditional manner

New York Sirloin – a king of Steaks, broiled to your selection of doneness. Regular cut or end cut... 6.50 / 7.95

Filet – this cut is famous for its tenderness ... 7.95

Teriyaki Steak – a juicy Sirloin marinated in Bartholomew's famous Teriyaki Sauce ... 7.50

Alaskan King Crab – 1 lb. of King Crab Legs with drawn butter ... mkt. price

Scampi – gently cooked in a lemon butter & garlic sauce ... 7.25

Fresh Seafood Specials
Your waitress will be pleased to tell you about today's Seafood Specials.

Daily House Specials
The chef each day prepares special offerings designed to please the palate. Please ask your waitress for today's Specials.

Salads
Bibb Lettuce, Romaine, Crisp Bacon with house dressing.

House Salad – Bibb lettuce, Romaine, baby shrimp, egg & chives.

Spinach Salad

Desserts
Creamy Cheesecake ... 1.50
Creme de Menthe, Rum or Cocoa parfait ... 1.75
French Ice Creams ... .95

Bartholomew's Liquored Coffees
1.95

Wines
	full	half
Rosé Waters	8.00	4.50
Pouilly Fuissé	12.00	6.00
Beaujolais	8.00	4.50

Carafes
glass 1.00 / half litre 2.95 / litre 3.75

Beverages coffee 50¢, tea 50¢, iced coffee or tea 75¢, milk 50¢
Soft drinks 50¢

sales tax will be added where applicable.

Westchester County: Banksville
LA CREMAILLERE
French $$

Cremaillère is the word for that great pot hook that suspends cooking utensils over a roaring fire. In Banksville, La Cremaillère means excellent French cuisine served in a beautiful Early American house, full of flowers and the bouquet of good wines. Its light, airy ambience, and food that is carefully prepared and served with pride are two reasons why this French country inn has maintained a high reputation over many years. Another reason is the wines. The management happily permits you to prowl through a large subterranean labyrinth where cool earthen-walled rooms are lined floor to ceiling with wine bins. This cellar contains a score of superb Bordeaux and Burgundies at prices most bibbers can afford and, for a kingly price, there are some treasures that were laid away before you and I were born. The food is quite delectable. Among the soups I've admired are cream of sorrel and cream of turnip, a hearty peasant delight. House specialties include *crêpes Cremaillère,* a delicious seafood-stuffed pancake; *côte de veau Normande,* veal chop with apples; and, in season, *salmis de faisan,* a ragout of pheasant. I also like their frankness in admitting that the English sole is frozen here. They have an outstanding pastry chef, and their coffee is exceptionally good. For a bucolic meal, fastidiously prepared, and a voyage through a cellar filled with old vintages, La Cremaillère is well worth a pilgrimage. Festive luncheons average about $12; satisfying dinners will be between $15 and $20. The restaurant is a few miles off Exit 31 on the Merritt Parkway, near the Connecticut border.

LA CREMAILLÈRE, Banksville, New York. Telephone: (914) BE4-3306. Hours: 12-2:30, 6-9:30, Tuesday-Saturday; 1-8, Sunday; closed Monday. Cards: AE, BA/Visa, CB, DC, MC. Reservations required. Parking lot. Full bar service.

Entrées

Poularde Rôtie aux Petits Légumes	9.25
Boeuf aux Carottes dans son Fond de Vin Rouge	11.25
Coquelet Sauté Veuve Brush (35 min.)	9.75
Pigeon Gustin, Purée de Navets	12.50
Curry d'Agneau Comptoir d'Inde	11.75
Côte de Veau Beauséjour	12.75
Ris de Veau aux Pommes Gourmandes	11.75
Rognons de Veau au Poivre Vert	9.75
Escalopines de Veau aux Olives de Nice	9.75
Caneton aux Fruits à l'Armagnac	11.75
Côte de Boeuf à la Moelle Pour 2	27.00

Ulster County: New Paltz
THE QUILTED GIRAFFE
French $$

The disease of suburbanitis far too frequently attacks restaurants outside of New York City and renders them subject to the hot on Tuesday, cold on Wednesday syndrome. The Quilted Giraffe, despite being tucked away in a little college town, really tries. When a waiter in a tuxedo greets you in a tiny village restaurant, isn't that trying? The Quilted Giraffe supports its image with pictures of giraffes everywhere and a stuffed namesake guards the cash register out front. There are many surprises on the menu, not all of them successful, but in a region of pizzas and Chinese-to-go, it is amazing how dedication to an ideal makes its mark. The owner personally scours Manhattan markets for the pick of fish, meats and vegetables. Meals are *prix fixe* at $19—high in the hinterlands, but not excessive considering what you get. *Canard au poivre des Isles* is blissfully fat-free duckling in a spicy green peppercorn sauce. *Filet de veau aux cèpes* is milk-fed veal touched with rosemary and thyme, served with wild mushrooms and a béarnaise sauce. *Tournedos au poivre* is another slightly peppery dish with a sauce *foyot* (an intense béarnaise) and the Stendahl Choice. There is a surprisingly thoughtful wine list and desserts are special.

THE QUILTED GIRAFFE, 3 Academy Street, New Paltz, New York. Telephone: (914) 255-9801. Hours: 5:30-10, Thursday-Tuesday; closed Wednesday. Cards: AE, BA/Visa, CB, DC, MC. Reservations required. Parking lot. Full bar service.

New Jersey: Tenafly
LE CHATEAU
French $$

Tucked away in Tenafly, an area not noted for gourmandizing, is a lovely little chalet, white and trim outside, light walls within, topped with auberge-like wooden beams. Downstairs the aura is more that of a tavern, upstairs that of an elegant country house. Two young couples run the place, and their kitchen brims with fine French cuisine. The owners have had good experience working in some of Manhattan's finest restaurants, and both food and service reflect this background. There are about 16 excellent choices on the *table d'hôte* dinner menu and everything I have sampled has been superior. *Canard à l'orange* is classically done, as is steak *au poivre*. Off the beaten track, and very prettily prepared, are items such as a delicate sole poached in champagne, *rognons de veau sautés au poivre vert*, veal kidneys with green peppercorns, and *côte de veau Château,* a sumptuous braised veal chop with chestnuts. Desserts are spectacularly good—creamier, lighter, more appealing to eye and palate than in many of the best Manhattan temples of *haute cuisine*. There is a carefully worked-out wine list. All in all, Le Château is suburban only in location; within its country charm resides a spirit of great sophistication. Luncheons average $7; dinners $13.50.

LE CHÂTEAU, 115 Country Road, Tenafly, New Jersey. Telephone: (201) 871-1500. Lunch: 12-2:30, Monday-Friday. Dinner: 6-10, Monday-Thursday; until 10:30, Friday-Saturday. Cards: AE, BA/Visa. Reservations suggested. Parking lot. Full bar service.

Index

MANHATTAN
*Dinner only
Aperitivo, 7
Arirang House, 8
Auberge Suisse, 10
Balkan Armenian, 12
Box Tree, 14
Cafe des Artistes, 15
Cafe du Soir, 16
Cafe Geiger, 18
Carlyle, 20
*Cellar in the Sky, 178
Charley O's, 22
Château Richelieu, 24
Chez Napoleon, 26
*Chez Pascal, 27
China Royal, 28
Christ Cella, 29
*Coach House, 30
Copenhagen, 32
*Coriander, 34
Crêpe Suzette, 36
Czechoslovak Praha, 38
David K's Chung Kuo Yuan, 40
Delicias Mejicanas, 120
Dezaley, 10
Divan Turkish Cuisine, 42
Eamonn Doran, 44
El Faro, 46
*El Parador, 48
Flower Drum, 50
Fondue Pot, 164
Four Seasons, 52
*Frankie & Johnnie's, 54
Gaylord, 56

Georges Rey, 58
Giambelli 50th, 60
Gian Marino, 62
Giordano, 64
Girafe, 66
Gloucester House, 68
Hermitage, 70
Hunam, 72
Hungaria, 74
Il Caminetto, 76
Iperbole, 78
Jack's Nest, 80
La Caravelle, 81
La Côte Basque, 82
La Folie, 84
La Grenouille, 86
La Petite Ferme, 88
Larre's, 89
Laurent, 90
Le Cirque, 92
Le Lavandou, 94
Le Madrigal, 96
Le Marmiton, 98
Le Perigord, 100
Le Perigord Park, 102
Les Pleiades, 104
Le Veau d'Or, 106
L'Olivier, 108
Lord (India), 110
Luchow's, 112
Lutece, 114
Madras Woodlands, 116
Main Street, 115
Maxwell's Plum, 118
Mayoor, 119

Mexi-Frost, 120
Mister Lee's, 122
Monsignore II, 124
Moon Palace, 126
Nippon, 128
Nirvana on Rooftop, 130
Orsini's, 132
Oyster Bar & Restaurant, 134
*Palace, 136
Palm Too, 138
Parkway, 140
Pavilion, 164
Peng's, 142
Puerta Real, 144
The Reidys', 146
Rio de Janeiro, 147
Roma di Notte, 78
Romeo Salta, 148
Rossoff's, 150
Russian Tea Room, 152
Sanctuary, 156
Sardi's, 154
Say Eng Look, 157
Sea Fare of the Aegean, 158
Siamese Gardens, 160
Sweets, 162
Swiss Center Restaurants, 164
Szechuan, 166
Sweets, 162
Swiss Center Restaurants, 164
Tandoor, 168
Torremolinos, 170
"21" Club, 172
Uncle Tai's Hunan Yuan, 174
*Vasata, 176
*Windows on the World, 178
Ye Waverly Inn, 181
Zapata's, 182

THE BRONX
Il Boschetto, 185

BROOKLYN
Gage & Tollner, 186
Peter Luger, 188

QUEENS
Cafe Valois, 194
La Boccaletta, 190
Villa Gaudio, 192
Zum Stammtisch, 193

LONG ISLAND
Arturo's, Belrose, 196
Cheong's Garden, West
 Hempstead, 198
Chi Ling, Cedarhurst, 198
La Goletta, Port Washington, 200
La Mansarde, Amityville, 202
L'Endroit, East Hills, 204
Little Park, Montauk, 206
Villa Pierre, Glen Cove, 208
Zanghi, Glen Cove, 210

PUTNAM COUNTY
The Arch, North Brewster, 211

ULSTER COUNTY
Quilted Giraffe, New Paltz, 216

WESTCHESTER COUNTY
Bartholomew's, Scarsdale, 212
Le Cremaillère, Banksville, 214

NEW JERSEY
Le Château, Tenafly, 217

MANHATTAN RESTAURANTS BY TYPE OF CUISINE

American
Coach House, 30
Frankie & Johnnies, 54
Jack's Nest, 80
Main Street, 115
The Reidys', 146
Rossoff's, 150
Sanctuary, 156
Ye Waverly Inn, 181

Austrian
Cafe Geiger, 18

Brazilian/Portuguese
Rio de Janeiro, 147

Chinese
China Royal, 28
David K's Chung Kuo Yuan, 40
Flower Drum, 50
Hunam, 72

Moon Palace, 126
Peng's, 142
Say Eng Look, 157
Szechuan, 166
Uncle Tai's Hunan Yuan, 174

Continental
Cafe des Artistes, 15
Carlyle, 20
Four Seasons, 52
Maxwell's Plum, 118
Sardi's, 154

Czechoslovakian
Czechoslovak Praha, 38
Vasata, 176

Danish
Copenhagen, 32

French
Cafe du Soir, 16
Château Richelieu, 24
Chez Napoleon, 26
Chez Pascal, 27
Crêpe Suzette, 36
Georges Rey, 58
Hermitage, 70
La Caravelle, 81
La Côte Basque, 82
La Folie, 85
La Grenouille, 86
La Petite Ferme, 88
Larre's, 89
Laurent, 90
Le Cirque, 92
Le Lavandou, 94
Le Madrigal, 96
Le Marmiton, 98
Le Perigord, 100
Le Perigord Park, 102
Les Pleiades, 104
Le Veau d'Or, 106
L'Olivier, 108
Lutece, 114
Palace, 136

German
Cafe Geiger, 18
Luchow's, 112

Greek
Seafare of the Aegean, 158

Hungarian
Hungaria, 74

Indian
Gaylord, 56
Lord (India), 110
Madras Woodlands, 116
Mayoor, 119
Nirvana on Rooftop, 130
Tandoor, 168

Indonesian
Lord (India), 110

International
Cellar in the Sky, 178
Coriander, 34
Eamonn Doran, 44
Mister Lee's, 122
"21" Club, 172
Windows on the World, 178

Irish
Charley O's, 22
Eamonn Doran, 44
The Reidys', 146

Italian
Aperitivo, 7
Giambelli 50th, 60
Gian Marino, 62
Giordano, 64
Girafe, 66
Il Caminetto, 76
Iperbole, 78
Monsignore II, 124
Orsini's, 132
Roma di Notte, 78
Romeo Salta, 148

Japanese
Nippon, 128

Jewish
Parkway, 140
Rossoff's, 150

Korean
Arirang House, 8

Mexican
Delicias Mejicanas, 120
El Parador, 48
Mexi-Frost, 120
Zapata's, 182

Middle Eastern
Balkan Armenian, 12
Divan Turkish Cuisine, 42

Roumanian
Parkway, 140

Russian
Russian Tea Room, 152

Seafood
Gloucester House, 68
Hermitage, 70
Oyster Bar & Restaurant, 134
Sea Fare of the Aegean, 158
Sweets, 162

Soul Food
Jack's Nest, 80

Spanish
El Faro, 46
Puerta Real, 144
Torremolinos, 170

Steaks/Chops
Christ Cella, 29
Frankie & Johnnie's, 54
Palm Too, 138
The Reidys', 146

Swiss
Auberge Suisse, 10
Dezaley's, 10
Fondue Pot, 164
Pavilion, 164

Thai
Siamese Gardens, 160

MANHATTAN RESTAURANTS SERVING SUNDAY BRUNCH
Cafe des Artistes, 15
Carlyle, 20
Charley O's, 22
Eamonn Doran, 44
Main Street, 115
Maxwell's Plum, 118
Windows on the World, 178
Ye Waverly Inn, 181

MANHATTAN RESTAURANTS OPEN UNTIL MIDNIGHT OR LATER
Box Tree, 14
Cafe des Artistes, 15
Cafe du Soir, 16
Cafe Geiger, 18
Charley O's, 22
Château Richelieu, 24
China Royal, 28
Coriander, 34
David K's Chung Kuo Yuan, 40
Eamonn Doran, 44
El Faro, 46
Frankie & Johnnie's, 54
Giambelli 50th, 60
Gian Marino, 62
Hungaria, 74
Iperbole, 78
La Côte Basque, 82
Maxwell's Plum, 118
Monsignore II, 124
Nirvana on Rooftop, 130
Orsini's, 132
The Reidys', 146
Russian Tea Room, 152
Sardi's, 154
"21" Club, 172

LET THESE GUIDES LEAD YOU TO THE BEST RESTAURANTS OF OTHER AREAS

The Best Restaurants of Chicago, Florida, Los Angeles, Pacific Northwest, San Francisco and Texas are described in these authoritative guides. Each is written by local food writers and critics. Each is the same size and format as *Best Restaurants New York,* with menus reproduced.

"This series . . . is designed to bring out the discriminating gourmet in everyone. We've found that many restaurant reviews contain more fancy prose than real meat and potatoes . . . so we're pleased to note that these reports have style *and* substance. . . . There's enough solid dining information in any of these guides to abolish the question 'Where can we eat tonight?' forever."
—The Travel Advisor

These books are available at bookstores in their respective areas or may be ordered directly from the publisher with the order form on the facing page.

STENDAHL WINE JOURNEYS

Each spring and fall Stendahl personally conducts visits through some of Europe's finest vineyards. For information on these tours, send this coupon to **Stendahl, Box A, Sea Cliff, New York 11579**

NAME _____

ADDRESS _____

CITY _____ STATE _____ ZIP_____

OTHER BEST RESTAURANT GUIDES

Best Restaurant guides to other areas are available in book stores. They may also be ordered directly from the publisher. Check the titles you wish and send with your check or money order to:
101 Productions, 834 Mission St., San Francisco, California, 94103. Please add 50 cents per book for postage and handling.

   Best Restaurants Chicago $2.95
   Best Restaurants Florida $2.95
   Best Restaurants Los Angeles & So. Calif. $3.95
   Best Restaurants New York $3.95
   Best Restaurants Pacific Northwest $2.95
   Best Restaurants San Francisco & No. Calif.
     $2.95
   Best Restaurants Texas $2.95

NAME _____

ADDRESS _____

CITY _____ STATE _____ ZIP_____

STENDAHL

Stendahl for many years has been a mentor to millions of New Yorkers on matters of food, restaurants and wine. *Dining with Stendahl,* a column of candid restaurant reviews, appears each Thursday in America's largest newspaper, the *New York Daily News.* For six years his radio broadcasts on wine and food were heard exclusively over WCBS-NY. Recently these radio essays have been syndicated to other stations across the country. He is currently completing two motion picture shorts, co-sponsored by Sabena Belgian World Airlines: "Wine Journey to Italy," and "Wine Journey to Alsace and Champagne." A cookbook on *Spicy Cooking Around the World* is scheduled for publication by Holt, Rinehart and Winston.

Stendahl has lectured on food and wine at the New School for Social Research. Soon his own Stendahl Center will open with advanced cooking courses, lectures by Stendahl on wines and cuisines of the world, and a series of wine-tasting seminars.

In 1978 Stendahl was the only American to receive the coveted *diplôme d'honneur de St. Vincent de Champagne* for "services rendered to the community of Champagne." He has also been made an honorary citizen of the Italian wine making village of Artimino in Tuscany.

Each spring and fall Stendahl personally escorts a group of wine lovers for private tastings in the best of European vineyards, plus special banquets in all-star restaurants. Tours include visits to Sicily, Italy, Germany and France. Additional information on these tours may be obtained by sending him the coupon on the reverse of this page.